WHAT THE CFO WANTS YOU TO KNOW

HOW YOU CREATE VALUE

CHARLES ASUBONTEN

outskirts
press

This book is dedicated to all the people in the various organizations and countries of the world that I have been privileged to work with over the years as the Chief Financial Officer (CFO) to create tremendous value.

You often tell me you have learned a lot from me; Well, I, too, have learned from you.

It is a symbiotic world; no person is an island.

Together, we create a better world!

Introduction and Acknowledgments

I WAS IN boarding school in Ghana when I did my first "IPO" (actually a blank check IPO – Initial Public Offering). I raised equity funds from school mates and teachers to start a school store.

One Friday evening, after we returned to campus from shopping wholesale all day to fill our inventory, it was announced that the Ghanaian currency was going to be changed the following Monday.

While most shopkeepers panicked and closed their stores for fear that they would lose money in the process, I decided that this was an opportunity to keep our shop operating.

When I ran the idea by one of the teacher board members, an art teacher at the school, he said it was a great idea. In fact, I always remember one thing he said: "This guy will become a great business man one day."

At the time I did not think much about it. I went ahead and made a huge profit from that event. After having worked in some of the best companies around the world, helping to create value for all stakeholders, and receiving similar comments, I have realized that this teacher gave me a great gift by praising what I thought was just the normal way of doing business. And for that I will be forever grateful to him.

His comment has spurred me on to make some bold business decisions which have created tremendous value along my CFO journey. Some of the bold initiatives I took at Rio Tinto were resisted, but in the end, tremendous value was created from them for the shareholders and all stakeholders. Rio Tinto is a global mining company headquartered in London. I had taken my accomplishments for granted until I returned to Phalaborwa (the town where Palabora Mining Company, the Rio Tinto subsidiary was located) in South Africa with my family for a vacation, from Zambia. When I went to the supermarket, people were calling my name all over and for a moment I felt like a rock star. I asked why and somebody said, "You helped people in town keep their jobs and created more jobs!" That is what I call value creation. I went back to Zambia with a new appreciation for the role of the CFO. I hasten to add that value creation in any enterprise is a team effort. I have always worked in a team to create value.

The one person who is behind these business improvement ideas and value creation that I have made around the world, and the one who deserves the utmost acknowledgment, is my mother. I learned entrepreneurship and more from her. The foundation for my creativity in business comes from working with her. That experience has always helped me to boil things down to their lowest common denominators. Creativity occurs when one is able to dismantle any transaction and look at their discrete parts, with the objective of what one is trying to accomplish in mind. It is easier to see linkages and find efficiencies in that manner.

She was a general merchandise trader, very pragmatic and she involved me in every facet of the business very early in my life. I learned sales, marketing and some light manufacturing, and eventually a lot of accounting and finance from her. I believe that she gave me my first CFO job. The question of nature versus nurture is always lurking at the back of any achievement. In this case, she can lay claim to both, and for that I am eternally grateful to her.

When I was an undergraduate student at North Carolina Central University in Durham, NC, I had the good fortune of doing an accounting summer internship at a pharmaceutical company, then called Burroughs-Wellcome, in the Research Triangle Park. It was the first company to develop an AIDS/HIV medicine. The drug was called AZT. Burroughs-Wellcome was also a predecessor company to what is now GlaxoSmithKline (GSK).

After helping the company set up a fixed asset system (working in a team of three, led by a Duke MBA student and another student from North Carolina State University[1]), we were given the opportunity to make a presentation to the finance leadership at the end of the summer.

My presentation was very well received. The next day, the

---

1 Fun fact – this student came from the same town in North Carolina where Andy Griffith, of the Andy Griffith show fame, came from – Mount Airy. We were regaled that summer with many tall tales! Now Barney....

controller, Jack Davis, told me that with my skills, I should go into public accounting, as he himself had been in public accounting and found it to be a good foundation for anybody going into finance.

It was some of the best advice I have received, as public accounting proved to be a sound foundation in global business. Jack was gracious enough to visit my school the following semester (upon my invitation) to share with me and my fellow business students his ideas about finance careers and what roles finance leadership plays in companies in value creation. Thank you, Jack.

I also want to thank a librarian at Burroghs-Wellcome who gave me a copy of Lee Iacocca's biography to read during that summer. I don't recall her name; perhaps I did not even know it at the time. Little did I know, at the time, that one day I would work at Ford Motor Company, let alone at Ford Product Development Finance (which was once referred to as the Marine Corps of Finance in Corporate America – Semper Fi). The book has helped me on my journey as I too have faced some of the issues that Lee Iacocca had to deal with at Ford Motor Company—perhaps not on the same scale, but there are similarities nonetheless along the value creation continuum. Iacocca, famously known as the father of the mini-van, was full of innovation and creativity. We both in our individual ways have challenged the status quo to create value. My interest in corporate governance came from that book. So, to that librarian, I say thank you.

When I joined Ford Motor Company, I was assigned a mentor, Peter Daniel. Originally from Australia, Peter had just arrived in the USA from Asia Pacific to work on a new vehicle program, the Lincoln luxury brands. Luckily for me, Peter is very strategic and process-oriented. After he realized that I was serious about business, he went to bat for me to get decent assignments on several occasions. Ford finance leadership has written about my legendary business acumen[2]. Peter, who retired as the Senior Vice-President and Corporate Controller from Ford, has been a great supporter of my career over the years. Even now, in retirement[3], he still offers me needed counsel. I can only say thank you, mate, for what you have done to help my career!

These acknowledgments will be incomplete without the

---

2   A supervisor at the Ford Product Strategy Office had this to say in my performance review: "He [Charles Asubonten], without exception, spots potential problems and suggests solutions that consider long-term implications."

3   When I was back in Dearborn during the summers for home visits from working overseas as CFO, Peter would invite me for lunch at the Glass House penthouse dining room, the original Henry Ford dining room! Coincidentally, I found out that my name in English is Ford! Had I known, maybe I would have stayed at Ford. After all, it is a company bearing my name, albeit in a different language. In one of those visits, Peter took me to the executive garage to look at the new Ford fleet (once a car guy, always a car guy), It was impressive. We ran into Allan Mullaly, the CEO of Ford, who wanted to know who I was. Speaking of Ford CEOs, when I first joined Ford Motor Company, I commuted over the weekends from Toledo, OH to Midland, MI. Once on my way back from Toledo to Midland, I stopped in Ann Arbor to check on my mailbox at the post office off of Plymouth Road (I had just moved away from Ann Arbor – so my mail was trailing). As I was emerging from the main doors, I saw a very nice Jaguar approaching the station. It turned out that it was Sir Alex Trotman (then CEO of Ford) and his wife, coming to check on their mailbox. They were coming from a Dr. Martin Luther King (MLK) Jr. event, as the day was an MLK holiday in the USA. We had a very pleasant chat.

mention of four professors from Ross School of Business at the University of Michigan, my graduate business school Alma Mater: Prof. Gunter Dufey, Prof. Priscilla Rogers, Prof. Noel Tichy, and Prof. Victor Bernard (of blessed memory).

Prof. Gunter Dufey has been more than a teacher to me. Not only did he impart some key global finance ideas that I have used over the years to create value in various companies, but he has also made provisions for me and my family in other ways as well. Prof. Dufey has also been very hospitable to me, whether in the USA or in Singapore. And for that I am eternally very grateful! I am also thankful indeed to his insightful and thoughtful partner, Prof. Priscilla Rogers who has always welcomed me and my wife, Rosiland, into their home. What a blessing she has been to us.

I met Prof. Noel Tichy during our MBA orientation in August 1992 when my cohorts and I were being introduced to global citizenship as part of the MBA program. He made an impact on me as he introduced the social aspects of leadership. He brought the founders of Focus: HOPE, Fr. Cunningham (a Roman Catholic priest) and Ms. Eleanor Josaitis to speak to our class, after we had spent all day cleaning some neighborhoods in Detroit. The pair founded Focus: HOPE in Detroit to provide needed assistance to people in Detroit during the hectic days after the riots. The event made an impact on me as I realized that in business, I could help make a difference with societal issues as well. I always remembered this encounter when I was serving as a board member of the Detroit Urban League.

I heard from Prof. Tichy again when he came to teach a class in Prof. Paula Caproni's Critical Organizational Challenges course. I remember clearly, even today, the work he had to do in the Appalachians to help the coal miners and the healthcare concerns in the region. I used to think about it when I was in mining, especially when it came to labor union issues. I got to know him better after I graduated and went back to attend his course on The Leadership Engine program in Ann Arbor, which was run in partnership with General Wayne Downing, former head of the U. S. Special Operations Forces.

After a full day of classes one day, we met in the Executive Education Lounge for some refreshments in the evening. After listening to my ideas all day of how to create value, one thing led to another, and he said to me: "Charles, you are our Jack Welch."[4] That has meant a lot to me, given that he was the first manager in charge of Jack Welch's in-house leadership academy at GE's Crotonville Leadership Development Center.

Shortly after the Executive Education Lounge comment by Prof. Tichy, a fellow parishioner at Divine Child Catholic Church in Dearborn, MI, handed me a copy of Jack Welch's interview with Geoff Colvin (then an editor at *Fortune* magazine) at the Sacred Heart University, after one weekday morning Mass. I had not met this parishioner before. He just handed me the tape and said: "I have this for you." After I watched it, I realized that the message would resonate with my teachings of value creation on the job.

Since then, I have shared the video or parts of it with my colleagues in Detroit, South Africa, Zambia, and Sacramento,

---

4   Coincidentally, among my cohorts at Ross School of Business, University of Michigan-Ann Arbor, somehow, I earned the nickname – "Kenichi Ohmae" the name of the author of "The Mind of the Strategist"; I suppose for my insightful comments in class!

just to name a few. Let me also say thank you to Mark Hurd, CEO of Oracle. I listened to one of his presentations on YouTube (I believe he was at NCR at the time) and instantly knew that he was a value-creator. I have used his presentations in my CFO Townhalls as well.

When I was working at DTE Energy in Detroit I remember one day, when the executive team was brainstorming about strategy on how to create value, it was my turn and I made some comments about how to approach capital spending. A president of one of the businesses who was chairing the session (I believe he was also the Chief Operating Officer of the whole company at the time) was sitting next to me. After my speech, he turned and patted me on the shoulder and said: "That was great!" This fellow was not known for back-slapping. He must have been moved greatly by what he heard. I tried to connect him with Prof. Tichy while I was at DTE. It is worth mentioning that in one of my early assignments at DTE Energy, I had co-led a strategy session with DTE Energy Office of the Presidents (OOPS as it was known) to advise on securitization of Fermi stranded costs and merger with MCN, major accomplishments which have led to tremendous value to DTE Energy shareholders.

One of the mantras I had when I got to Palabora was: "Every Business is a Growth Business" – the title of a book by Prof. Tichy and Prof. Ram Charan (whose book titled *What the CEO Wants You to Know* inspired me to write this book *What the CFO Wants You to Know*). I believe that "Every Business is a Growth Business," so much so that I even encouraged the CEO at Rio Tinto in London at the time I was working at Palabora to read the book. Thank you, Prof. Tichy, for all you have given through writing and counsel.

In some ways, you can say that to be referred to as Jack Welch (early in your career) by your former professor who worked with Jack Welch is akin to a MacArthur Award (without the cash). For that I am very grateful.

That Jack Welch comparison from Prof. Tichy has propelled me in my quest to create value over the years. Across geographies, men and women of goodwill have recognized my expertise in this area. I have also tried my best to share my knowledge everywhere I have been. I believe we make the world a better place when we share knowledge to increase or improve our well-being. Thank you to Keith Marshall[5], Mo Marshall, Dennis Brazier, Niesje Reynecke, and Mari (du Plessis) Oosthuizen, who even joined in on my value-creation quest in Zambia on the Copperbelt (after our work in Palabora).

Now let me speak of the late Prof. Victor Bernard. He taught me a course in company valuation in my last semester in the MBA program. After one of the classes, he asked me

---

[5] Keith Marshall was the CEO who hired me to join him in Palabora to create value. As he put it, he and I were the dynamic duo! After one presentation to the analysts in Cape Town at the Mount Nelson hotel, he turned to me and said: "Charles, you and I are great value-creators!" I'll never forget Keith's question to me, the first night we met. After dinner at the W'Sens, the French restaurant in London, opposite the Sofitel Hotel in St. James, he turned to me and said: "You look very polished, do you think you will like the mining environment, with all its dirt?" Instantly I said: "Well, Keith from the earth I came and to the earth I shall return." He kept quiet for a moment. I bet that was the moment he decided that I was the guy for the job. I believe I got help for that answer; it was not long after Lent. Of course, the Church had reminded me of my humanness from Ash Wednesday: "From the earth you came and to the earth, you shall return." Thank you, Keith, for putting the trust in me to help Palabora create tremendous value for all shareholders, including Rio Tinto and Anglo American.

to come by his office to speak with him. When I met him, he asked me if I had considered getting a PhD. This is what he said: "You seem different from other MBA students; you appear to be genuinely interested in learning and using that knowledge for something meaningful." That's one of those moments that you are astonished and then you are reminded of the famous Abraham Lincoln quote: "You can fool all the people some of the time and some of the people all the time, but you cannot fool all of the people all of the time." Some people pay attention and they can tell who is who[6]. After I got past my shock, I told him that yes, I had. He said that I should consider it seriously. I shared my reluctance with him—that I had been away in school getting an MBA, while my spouse lived in Midland, MI about two hours away (Rosiland had agreed to stay and work for Dow Chemical, as it was difficult for trailing spouses to get jobs in their fields in Ann Arbor). He told me about his own family situation (what they were going through at the time) and he told me to think about the PhD for a year and if I were still interested, I was to come to see him that time. He willingly said that he could be my advisor. He told me what to do to be ready for the program (relating to research and academic journals); for a long time, I kept the yellow paper he wrote on. Well, before the year would be up, he suddenly passed away one day jogging with his colleagues from the university. I have always cherished that conversation and kindness, he showed. I am forever grateful. May his soul continue to rest in peace. While the PhD question came up from others afterwards, I did not pursue it, as I was more interested in running companies.

---

6   Similar nice compliments would later be made to me by a DTE Energy CFO, Larry Gerberding, when I went to say goodbye to him when he was retiring.

Speaking of Ross School of Business, I met Vincent Harris on the first day of our MBA orientation. A Californian, Vincent had gone to Berkeley for his undergraduate degree. He and I had several conversations during our stay in Ann Arbor. He has done a remarkable job of keeping in touch over the years. He has sent me many inspirational words even when I was at the "ends of the earth," working in mining. As it turned out, he had been posted to Sacramento when I arrived to take my post as the CFO of CalPERS. Vincent has been God-sent, as he has provided me with some needed counsel in Sacramento. Let me say a big thank you to Vincent, who has been part of my journey in many ways.

I would like to acknowledge Guy Elliott, the former CFO and Finance Director at Rio Tinto. He gave me a lot of encouragement while I was at Rio. Many times, it felt like he was the only one in London who understood what I was doing to create value at Palabora or genuinely concerned about my career welfare. Guy wrote me a very encouraging note after I hosted him for a Rio Tinto southern Africa finance leadership meeting at the InterContinental Hotel at the Oliver Tambo Airport in Johannesburg. Guy and I made a presentation to the financial analysts in Johannesburg during the same visit, when the board and leadership team of Rio Tinto came on an operational tour of Africa. I benefited greatly from his counsel. Guy – thanks for all that you do.

Finally, my thanks go to my life partner and a former classmate. She has been with me through thick and thin as I have worked to create value in various organizations and countries. South Africa was going through the polls to choose their first democratic leader in 1994 when I was graduating from the

MBA program. I remember saying to Rosiland that one day we would go to South Africa. She asked why, and I said I didn't know[7]. But as it turned out, we did. I appreciated her sense of adventure of moving the whole family from Dearborn to Phalaborwa.

If there is an advanced diploma in global logistics, I believe that she has earned one, with distinction! I am eternally grateful for her support, encouragement, and love. Thank you, Rosiland; I would not be here without your help.

Charles A Asubonten, CPA, CFA
Sacramento, CA
November 8, 2018

---

7 When I was working at DTE Energy years later after the comment to Rosiland, my assistant gave me a Nelson Mandela's book *Long Walk to Freedom*. At the time, I had no plans suggesting that I was going to South Africa someday. In fact, when I got to South Africa, one of the first gifts I got was the same book. I did not get the chance to read it until I had an unscheduled weekend in Namibia, when I went downstairs at the hotel and bought a copy. I returned to South Africa with a renewed sense of what Nelson Mandela had done for South Africa's independence. I had earlier admired him for his views on all races when I read Robben Island in high school. He did not want whites to be thrown into the sea. Indeed, he wanted democracy for all people. We labeled my first earnings report at Palabora "Long walk back to profitability."

TABLE OF CONTENTS

PREFACE

MY PURPOSE IN writing this book is to inform the reader what a CFO does to create value. One thing I have learned in my career is that people easily lose sight of what business is all about and how to measure success and create value. This book is for everyone, even CFOs. By going through it and following the ideas here, you too can create or help create tremendous value. Value creation occurs when the value of a business' output far exceeds its costs. These concepts will be explained throughout the book.

As you probably just read from my background, I learned business acumen very early in life. I shall share a simple way of acquiring business acumen in this book as you learn from the value-creator CFO.

Every organization has a CFO or somebody who is performing a function akin to what a CFO does. The CFO's role is very important when it comes to value creation, making money (cash). Because of the simple fact that, it is the only role in the organization that cuts across all functions and at the same time is responsible for the financial well-being of the whole enterprise. Money is the lifeblood of all organizations. Companies need money to stay in business. Of course, money is needed to pay for employees' services, including yours and mine. I am very interested in value creation, as I suspect that you are too or hopefully you will be, after reading this book.

Luck or great timing helps in life. As the late President Ronald Reagan once quipped: "I would rather be lucky than smart." Warren Buffet has said that being in a business on the upswing makes one look very smart. On the other hand, value creation is not alchemy; you cannot put in base metals and find gold as your output! Even with luck, you still have to know the basics of value creation to achieve the optimal level.

I have seen times when the prices of a company's products or services are at their zenith, and yet the company was floundering on the stock market. My argument is that the management team did not have a CFO who knew how to create value. As you will see, it takes more than skill. There is a certain level of leadership, creativity, and innovation involved in delivering tremendous value. The CFO must be a catalyst to help put all the tools at the disposal of the entity to create value. In some companies, the Chief Executive Officer (CEO) plays this role but the CFO's role is one that can act as a back stop to ensure that somebody is playing this role.

Rising tides lift all boats but the boats must be on the water or close to shore, not far away on land, to be lifted. And so, it is with value creation. A concerted effort, usually led by the CFO, must be put in place to achieve the value desired. It works better if the CEO is a value-creator person and has a CFO who possesses the requisite knowledge and expertise to make it happen. Being a CFO is like being a pilot. You have to be trained in the necessary skills and intuitively understand the linkages in business to create tremendous value or as Malcolm Gladwell puts it: "You need to put in your 10,000 hours" to become an expert. I believe that if one puts in those hours, one gets equipped to have the necessary background for creativity and innovation required to create value. Most activities include some amount of risk-taking. Having enough exposure to many facets of business and life will improve one's chances of taking risks which can lead to better payoffs.

It is advantageous for you and your CFO to know what needs to be done to create value. Everybody in a company plays a part in value creation. Remember your future or your pension depends on it. Value creation is more than beating the competition. It is the art and science of generating the returns that are better and above how much it costs your company to run its business.

As you have probably heard before, knowledge is power. Whichever side you are on—whether you work for a CFO, thinking about working in the CFO's group or just wanted to have general knowledge as an employee or potential employee—I want to share my knowledge with you so that you will be well-prepared to understand the CFO's function. Every CEO should make this book a required reading for all their employees. The book will serve as a refresher for anyone who needs to brush up on the basics of value creation. It'll also help explain why certain CFOs create value and others don't. I have tried to keep it light and yet with some substance. My hope is that as you get interested, you will follow up on the ideas and terms introduced here, as I'll provide sufficient reference for those who desire to take this to the next level.

I have spent a good amount of my time learning how to create value. When I first got the chance to be a CFO of a listed public company, I helped that company increase the value of their shares more than five times, among other achievements. Before that, I had helped the leadership of Dow Chemical Company, Ford Motor Company, and DTE Energy, among others, to create substantial value. The interesting part about value creation is that it is not limited to publicly traded companies or geographies or even business. Value can be created anywhere once you understand the purpose of the organization and set out to get the appropriate combinations to achieve desired outcomes.

Not-for-profit organizations also benefit from the services of a CFO who has an eye for value creation and embeds the tools of value creation in the decision-making process. Value creation begets efficiency, and efficiency begets a well-run entity! A well-run entity is good for all stakeholders. During my tenure as CFO of CalPERS, I set out to bring in these tools to help the organization in its quest to meeting beneficiaries' retirement and healthcare needs.

One thing to keep in mind as you read this book is that it may begin to sound repetitive, but when it does, remember that the tools and strategies to create value are repetitive; they are reinforcing, and circular. It is only when the linkages are considered and managed well that an organization can create value. The purpose, people, and processes all have to work in tandem to achieve optimal value for the enterprise.

I would recommend this book for everyone who is affiliated or will be affiliated with a CFO at some point in their lifetime. These ideas are not limited to one geography. With some modifications, they can be applied in China, Japan, India, or even on continents; Europe, the Americas, Australia, and Africa.

I wish you all the best as you embark on this journey. Thank you for giving me the opportunity to accompany you on your professional endeavors.

— I —
PURPOSE OF THE
ORGANIZATION

1

———✺———

How Every Entity
is Organized

IT IS WORTHWHILE to point out at the outset that every entity must have a purpose. That purpose should be obvious to everybody in the organization. Some businesses exist to make profit (money) and provide good returns (in the form of dividends or buy-backs) for their shareholders, after paying for the costs of doing business which include paying for your salary, benefits, and the cost of the funds used in the business.

Other organizations exist to fulfill a mandate; a social purpose. The California Public Employees' Retirement System (CalPERS), the largest pension system and the second-highest healthcare purchaser in the United States of America (USA), is an entity of the State of California government operations, responsible for providing pension benefits and healthcare for public employees and retirees (and their beneficiaries) whose employers sponsor the system.

From the articles of incorporation or the documents that set out the purpose of the organization, you can learn how the organization is to be managed or run (you can usually find this from the company secretary or the legal office).

In almost all instances, as the case may be for your organization, there is a governing body which is sometimes referred to as the Board of Directors (for businesses) or Board of Trustees (usually for not-for-profit entities). The board works with the management team to develop the strategy for the entity (the board must approve the strategy). The strategy lays out how to achieve the purpose (or mission of the entity).

The board then delegates most of the authority (power) on how to achieve the mission to the CEO, who in turn forms a management team (sometimes with the approval of the board) to run the day-to-day operations. One key individual in the management structure is the CFO.

In many instances, this individual is a Certified Public Accountant (CPA) and in some cases has obtained advanced degrees and other credentials germane to the function of the CFO. The CFO is responsible for running all the financial affairs of the entity.

Even though the CEO has the utmost responsibility for your organization, the CFO is the individual charged with the responsibility of ensuring financial adequacy and independence for your organization. One might even dare say that this individual's role is to ensure the longevity of the organization. For this reason, the CFO must be a rational individual, not given into frivolous thinking and planning. It helps tremendously if they are disciplined individuals, as many of the functions of the role require discipline and diligence.

Even countries have CFOs. In some countries, the incumbent is often referred to as the Finance Minister, in others such as the USA or the United Kingdom (UK), they are called the Secretary of the Treasury and the Chancellor of the Exchequer, respectively. In some respects, Alexander Hamilton[8] remains the quintessential CFO. As the first United States Secretary of the Treasury, he was an architect of many of the US financial systems we take for granted today. My ideas on how to create value are applicable to roles of the finance ministers as well. If they follow the ideas as discussed here, they too can lift their countries to economic prosperity. The finance function is similar across all entities.

In all human events, there is a need for somebody to be keeping an eye on the finances. Legend has it that Judas was the CFO during Jesus' time (Scripture says that among the Apostles, he kept the purse, which is the equivalent to what the modern-day CFO does). Whether he created value or not, I think the theologians can help us with that question.

The point is that every organization needs a CFO, even the church (which is exhorted to leave pecuniary matters to Caesar. But there must be a conduit: presto – CFO! as there has to be some accounting to Caesar – paying taxes). Depending on the organization, the title may be different, but the roles performed would be similar.

---

8   The Alexander Hamilton Award by the Treasury & Risk magazine recognizes individuals and companies for their innovation in the treasury and financing spaces.

In any event, the CFO and CEO must work together as the CEO leads the vision and purpose of the organization. The CFO has to ensure that things run smoothly and that the CEO's strategy is backed up with realistic financial assumptions. Somebody said it better: *the CFO should all be about facts and numbers.* From my experience, the CFO helps create value, if a qualified CFO is hired and allowed to do what needs to be done.

The CFO's staff usually includes a controller, treasurer, a risk manager, and others such as head of Information Technology (IT), Supply Chain, Internal Audit or Legal or Company Secretary. The roles differ from organization to organization, as the staff is usually organized around the mandate and the needs of the organization. However, to gear up the company for value creation, certain organizational structures lend themselves easily to the mandate (we shall discuss later).

In some countries (as in European countries and other places) both the CEO and CFO serve on the board of directors. Those CFOs have the additional title of Finance Director (not to be confused with the Director of Finance position for junior executives in the USA) In the USA, it is usually only the CEO who serves on the board of directors, mostly as its Chairman also (or Chairperson). The CFO also serves as a conduit to the Audit Committee[9]. The Audit Committee per-

---

9 As part of my CFO continuing education, I took the National Association of Corporate Directors and Financial Executives International seminar entitled: "Rules of the Road: What Boards Expect from the CFO" in Washington DC on December 1, 2004. I met the Honorable JC Watts from Oklahoma, who was also attending the same course. I got the opportunity to talk shop with him. I noticed that he later served on the International Transmission Company (ITC) 's board. I was involved in

forms an important role for the board, ensuring that among other things, that the books and records are kept with integrity by management.

SUMMARY

Organizations are formed with a purpose and structure.

The CFO is the one person in the organization who must make sure that all financial matters are taken care of prudently and that the organization is working to create value for all stakeholders. This is a balancing act that requires expertise and certain personality traits.

Ask Yourself

1. Do I know how my company or entity is organized?
2. Have I read the articles of incorporation or founding document of my entity?

---

spinning off the transmission business from DTE Energy, which became ITC.

2

UNDERSTANDING THE PURPOSE OF YOUR ORGANIZATION

WHEN I WAS teaching at Wayne State University in Detroit and at the University of Michigan – Dearborn, I impressed upon my students to find out the purpose of any endeavor they are involved in or will be involved in, whether it be a company, a class, or a meeting.

I know that in the real world, it is not always easy or possible to ascertain every purpose. However, it is important to at least try to find out the purpose in any situation. Inherent in the purpose will be the strategy to achieve the purpose. To put it another way, the purpose will lend itself to a cogent strategy to achieve the same. Without knowing the strategy, you won't have a fighting chance of success.

When you find out the purpose of the entity, your job becomes easier, as you will know what is expected of you. In the same way, you must try to understand why your organization exists and what it is trying to accomplish. This helps you to know the purpose of your department, your specific job, and how it fits into the big scheme of things in the entity.

For example, in my career at Ford Motor Company, Ford's mission then was to become: "The world's leading consumer company providing automotive goods and services." When I served as the CFO of CalPERS, our mission was to "deliver retirement and health care benefits to members and their beneficiaries." Those are simple missions that all employees should know and keep front and center, as they go about performing their daily assignments.

In the two instances just described, your CFO would like you to know that there is a need for results in order to achieve those objectives. That is where value creation comes into the picture. Resources are needed, in both instances, to run the organizations. In addition, shareholders and retirees expect returns for their investments and efforts, respectively. Without delivering results or returns, there won't be resources. And that is the fastest way to make an organization irrelevant.

In the example of Ford Motor Company, resources are needed to build stamping and assembly plants. These are capital investments or expenditure, often referred to as capex. Resources are needed for engineering and designing to occur before the building of the products.

While the capital investment involved in not-for profit entities like CalPERS can be minimal, they still need resources to perform the functions required to achieve their purpose. Specifically, investment in technology, logistics, and the like must still be made to ensure that the organizations function as required, and in keeping with the times.

Employees will have to be paid for joining Ford and assisting in its mission of vehicle production. Such operating spending or expenditure for revenue generation is referred to as opex. Before the product is bought and shipped to the customer, there will be sales, marketing, and distribution expenses, such as paying the transportation companies which send the finished vehicles to the dealerships.

All these expenses are part of the costs for Ford Motor Company to achieve its goal of producing and selling vehicles. Ford then receives revenues or sales income after the product is sold (in the real world, it does not always happen that way, as companies such as Dell Computers receive payment upfront, even before the computer is manufactured).

In a similar way, at CalPERS, the system must determine the costs for paying the pension of the employees *when* they retire and *actually paying* those who have retired.

They then send a bill to the employers who have sponsored the employees (let's bear in mind that employees also contribute toward their retirements as well), then when CalPERS receives payments (from the two sources) it invests the money by buying stocks, bonds, real assets (real estate and infrastructure) and other investments, sometimes referred to as alternative investments, usually private equity, and hedge funds. The returns from these investments help to meet the payments to retirees and beneficiaries. The commingled funds also support the running of the operations, to the tune of about $1.6 billion annually.

FIG 1

How are CalPERS Retirement Benefits Funded?

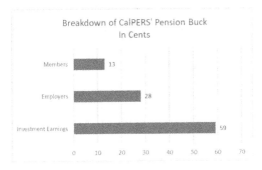

Breakdown of CalPERS' Pension Buck
In Cents

Members	13
Employers	28
Investment Earnings	59

0 10 20 30 40 50 60 70

Source: CalPERS

Fig 1 is a breakdown of what is referred to as the CalPERS' Pension Buck. The chart shows that as of June 2018, CalPERS' cashflow over the last 20 years demonstrated that every dollar spent on public employees' pensions came from the following sources:

Investment earnings: 59¢
Employer contributions 28¢
Member contributions 13¢

Said differently, 59% of the retiree payments come from investments, while employer contributions and member contributions make up 28% and 13% respectively of retiree benefits.

Healthcare is a little different, in that for the most part, the employers and employees pay for the costs on a Pay-As-You-Go (PAYGO) basis.

In this case, the CFO would have to make sure that prudent investments, billings, and collections are being made to maintain or improve the attribution above and also be able to support the operations for both pensions and healthcare

Your CFO would like you to know what happens in your specific company. If these processes (the operating cycle that your entity goes through to accomplish its mission) are not known to you, please follow up with your CFO organization to learn about them (knowing this information will help in the value-creation efforts). I urge CFOs to make sure that every employee understands how its entity creates value. Simply put, sharing this information with all employees is almost mission accomplished for value creation. Once employees are informed, they go the extra mile to capture all efficiencies for the organization to win the value creation process.

One thing that should be getting clear to you at this point is that every organization needs resources to accomplish its mission and satisfy the shareholders and all stakeholders, as stated already. The resources are utilized to meet the mandate or the purpose of that organization. As an employee, your CFO needs you to understand the purpose of the organization, the resources needed to run the organization, how the resources are obtained, and how to use those resources efficiently to achieve the purposes and aims of the organization. I bring this up here again because there are many facets to it, and we'll look at it again when we discuss the financial aspects of the CFO's role.

All entities are pretty much the same, in that they have to focus on generating cash, paying attention to margins, (even in the case of not-for-profit entities), targeting growth opportunities, ensuring healthy returns on assets (deploying the capital invested in the business for better returns than what they cost) and making sure that they are taking good care of their customers and/or stakeholders. Financial analysts usually refer to these questions as the fundamentals of the entity.

I mentioned discipline. A good CFO keeps tabs on their analyses (more to come on this later in the book) to ensure that the organization has what it needs to grow. Let me point out here something which bedevils some CFOs: the key to the organization's survival is good growth (or profitable growth). Therefore, the CFO does not have to be Mr. No or Mrs. No all the time[10]. Some CFOs get on a power high and will say "No" to every spending request from operations. The CFO must have a good business sense to know when to say "No," and when to encourage spending[11]. The saying in Detroit[12] was that the engineers liked to design and build fancy mouse traps, so finance had to be on hand to stop them. I don't subscribe to that and the value-creator CFO needs to dialogue with the engineers to understand and join in when the potential growth far exceeds the cost. This is one of the reasons why I have

---

10 Don't get me wrong; I believe in organizational discipline to control budgets and targets (it has been my job!), however when it comes to growth or ideas for growth – dialogue is always ideal. As in that old GM commercial – "That's what happens when finance and operations do lunch."

11 While writing this book, I am reading an interesting book called *Autonomy* by Lawrence D. Burns and Christopher Shulgan. Mr. Burns was once the GM Corporate Vice President for Research, Development and Planning. There is a quote in the book from Rick Wagoner, former GM CEO: "We can go bankrupt by running out of money, or bankrupt by not being technologically relevant." The value-creator CFOs take this quote to heart as they straddle a balance to ensure that the enterprise is viable today, while working to secure its future viability by making prudent investments.

12 You have probably heard it said before that Detroit's (the automotive industry's) downfall was due to people who understood finance but not vehicles or manufacturing. I think the jury is still out! But for the value-creator CFO, they need to know both, and very well, as this book argues.

also been interested in producing finance education for non-finance managers, so that we all could be "singing from the same hymn book," so to speak.

The CFO wants you to know that good customer relationships are good for business. Better customer relationships lead to repeat business. Repeat business can be very good, especially if the margin is healthy. The same thing can be said for not-for-profit organizations. Shareholders and stakeholders are happy when they get value for money!

Margin is the difference between what the customer pays and how much it costs the company to produce and sell the product or service. You have probably heard different terms like gross margin and net margin. Let's keep it simple and just focus on the term margin – which is really another word for profit, if we lump all expenses together, including taxes.

The number of times that a company creates this margin is referred to as its velocity (that is how long it takes from production, or raw inputs, to sales of its products or services). That is how often a product or service is sold. The return your company earns, over the cost of money used, depends on the margin and velocity[13].

Think of the grocery store, which does not make a lot of profit on a transaction but has a high velocity as more customers keep shopping day in and day out. The grocer restocks the shelves, and the customers return to buy them as they need the "essential commodities." The grocery stores stay in business

---

13 This is a very important concept that if you want more information on it, I would refer you to *Every Business Is a Growth Business* by Ram Charan and Noel M. Tichy

making money, but a little bit at a time, which sometimes grows to be big over a long period of time (not all the times though).

No matter the department that you are in, understanding the key facts of how your company operates or creates value (makes money or does an efficient job with the resources that they use) will allow you to do your best, and be promoted as fast as possible, and feel good about yourself as you contribute to this achievement.

The key to understanding your company is to hang on to this concept of margin and velocity. It is very easy to get bogged down in details and lose sight of what your entity is trying to achieve, as the company gets larger and complexities abound. However, if you keep this simple concept in mind, you will always have the business acumen to address the important issues needed to create value in your organization. Your CFO would like you to know that no matter where you work in the organization, you have a key role to play in the entity's value-creation process.

My favorite example is the mailroom. If you work in the mailroom and work efficiently, the costs of running that mailroom will be smaller than otherwise. In companies where receiving manual checks is still part of the operations (assuming that automation and cyberoperations haven't been introduced yet), delivering checks quickly to banks for clearing will cut down the cost of working capital for the company. Indeed, mailroom employees have a key role to play in advancing the company's mission of creating value.

You have probably heard companies talk about creating

shareholder value. In the case of for-profit companies, the company creates value when it earns more money than how much it costs to operate. It must be noted that a company can be profitable and struggle to make "money" – less cash than what it has to pay for the money used in the business. We'll talk more about that later. For not-for-profit entities, value is created when fewer resources are used to achieve the purpose or mission of the organization and beneficiaries are satisfied (and it has a surplus or expenses met with available resources – no deficits). Stakeholders refer to this as a win-win situation. Their needs are met, and the organization is financially sound.

SUMMARY

Every organization has a purpose. They are there to serve stakeholders. Businesses strive to create value for shareholders. Not-for-profit organizations create value when they achieve win-win solutions for all stakeholders. To create value, everyone associated with the entity needs to know how the company creates value and what role they are required to play.

Ask Yourself

1. How does my company create value?
2. Where is my department in the value-creation chain of the company?

3

THE ROLE OF THE CFO

DEPENDING ON WHERE you work, you may not get to see the CFO as often as you will see the other executives or even the CEO. In fact, for a long time, the CFO was in charge mostly of the back-office stuff, but not anymore. Before I say anything further about the CFO and how they are viewed in various organizations, let me provide in a nutshell the duties of the CFO who can help create value in your organization.

For an organization to create value and focus on its mission, the role of the CFO is crucial. The CEO, to whom the CFO reports, is usually operating on several fronts: dealing with people issues, government, regulators, and the media, among others. One hears about the CEO of the company creating value but not necessarily the CFO. Nevertheless, Warren Buffet would tell you that he has been able to create value over the years through his "partnership" with his CFO, Charlie Munger. CFOs are usually known by their works, not by publicity. All great CEOs—the likes of Jack Welch of GE, Sam

Walton of Walmart, Andy Grove of Intel—have always been surrounded by a great partner, a knowledgeable and able CFO. These CFOs have helped their companies create "moat" (a competitive advantage over other companies), to borrow a word from Warren Buffet.

So, while the CEO has the ultimate responsibility for creating value, the CFO is the one who leads the organization in the value-creation efforts. A leader's most important role is to create value for all stakeholders. A value-creator CFO brings unique skills that extend beyond the traditional role of a CFO – producing financial reports (or what some people refer to as number-crunching). This value-creator CFO does more than that, as we'll see in this book. There are also certain enablers that must be in place for the CFO to create value. The organizational setup should be one that lends itself readily to value creation. I am specifically speaking of a matrix organization where the CFO's role is fully embedded in the organization. A matrixed CFO organization has leaders in various parts of the organization who can act as "integrators" and provide active voice for all. The value-creator CFO who is a strategic business partner must have direct reports who also work with all parts of the enterprise.

The value-creator CFO looks more into the future to see how the business can create value with the resources at its disposal. This function is in sharp contrast to the image of CFOs of previous eras who were deemed to be back-office number-crunchers. The value-creator CFO is avant-garde in many respects; hence, the need for a balancing act. They are still responsible for ensuring that controls are in place and that all rules and regulations are followed. The value-creator

CFO has to be a business strategist with a very strong finance background.

FIG 2

Summary of the CFO's Responsibilities:

1) Corporate strategy (or strategic planning)

2) Financial strategy

3) Budgeting, management control, and risk management[14]

4) Financial management[15]

The value-creator CFO focuses on the above four areas to create value all at once; as they are in self-reinforcing, feed-forwarding, and feedback loops

---

14 This is what I referred to in the book as "Developing the Price Tag." And this should result in expected value differential for the enterprise, which may be positive or negative after the annual budgeting process. In other words, value must be assessed after this exercise.

15 This is what I write about under "CFO Maintenance."

To add value, the CFO must:

1. Be intimately involved in the corporate strategy (or strategic planning as it is sometimes referred to, especially in the not-for-profit sector), working hand-in-hand with the executive leaders of the organization for a common understanding of what the organization wants to achieve.

2. Lead the financial strategy – which is how the organization will function financially, end to end, to get to its end goal. That is working on a strategy for its capital structure and how to achieve the returns over and above the cost of capital used in the business.

3. Focus on budgeting and management control. As part of the financial process, this is where the CFO puts systems and procedures in place consistent with the financial strategy.

4. Provide the highest level of financial management. This involves the day-to-day rigor required to achieve the organizational financial goals.

In essence, the CFO must be a versatile individual and be able to exert a lot of influence and collaboration to be a value-creator. The value-creator CFO is a change agent and a source of competitive advantage for their firm at once.

That was exactly what I did when I was assigned to Palabora Mining Company in South Africa[16]. I worked with the leader-

16 Shortly after my arrival at Palabora, the current President of South Africa, Cyril Ramaphosa and associates from Metorex (a mining company which, I believe, has since folded) paid us a visit as they were looking for a fire sale of Palabora. That visit strengthened our resolve, as we believed that there was still value in Palabora to be reaped!

ship team and the executive committee, to set out a company strategy; we put emphasis on businesses that were cash rich, took away resources from businesses which were not incrementally adding to cash (in other words, they were draining cash from the other businesses), increased spending on projects with excess payoffs, and organized an investor presentation on October 6th 2006 to lay out our strategy to investors. By October 19th, 2006, the share price had risen by 25%, as was reported by Bloomberg.[17] For the next three years, I worked with members of the executive committee to execute and course-correct as we had communicated[18] to investors.

---

17 Palabora Shares Surge After Presentation on Expansion, Bloomberg, October 19th, 2006

18 Granted, Palabora was a turnaround case. However, any value-creator CFO should have these "checklist" items in place when they assume office. I have replicated this approach elsewhere, when the situation was not as dire as it was in Palabora.

Fig 3

The Asubonten CFO Value-Creation Hierarchy

As in the Summary of the CFO responsibilities in Fig 2, the pyramid and the inverted pyramid numbers in Fig 3 show the CFO's responsibilities as follows:

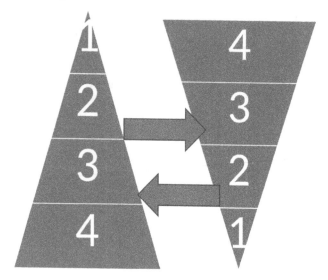

1) Corporate strategy (or strategic planning)
2) Financial strategy
3) Budgeting, management control, and risk management
4) Financial management

In essence, the CFO's work will look like the pyramids in Fig 3 as they focus on the strategy at the top of the pyramid to the left, while at the same time, financial management sits at the top of the value- creation effort in the pyramid to the right. In the Asubonten CFO Value-Creation Hierarchy, just like Maslow's Hierarchy in psychology, for the organization to create value, the financial- management portion serves as the foundation to provide the "safety and security" needed in the organization for value creation. Without that "safety and security" foundation provided by sound financial management, actualization, which in this case is the enterprise's value being recognized by investors and other stakeholders, success may elude the organization. Therefore, in this value creation model, financial management and the corporate strategy both form interchangeably the base and apex of the value-creation system. The CFO has to ensure that the organization is the most efficient in its financial operations. Such financial hygiene will permeate the organization and serve as a foundation for the "strategy" thinking at the highest levels of the organization.

In simpler terms, I worked with the team to assess the potential of the company, using an in-house valuation model[19], developed a multi-pronged plan of action, developed talent (especially in the finance organization), and created a results-oriented and high-performing teams across the organization. We tried to put the CFO group in tip-top shape. After all, it is said that she who seeks equity must come with clean hands. I believe that that is very important for the CFO to create value. The CFO needs to set an example in efficiency in their own shop, so that he can expect the same from the rest of the organization. This is what I referred to as the Financial Management in the "Asubonten CFO Value-Creation Hierarchy." In the end, we made the equity which was already in the business sweat for more cash. We needed it; the company was on the brink of bankruptcy.

Regardless of the organization, the CFO will be responsible for working with the senior management team and others to

---

19 This was a Discounted Cash Flow (DCF) model. The DCF model has been known to be the best predictor of value as it incorporates both returns and growth prospects.

create and refine the strategy of the entity. Sometimes, there is a strategy leader who also reports directly to the CEO. To create value, the CFO and this individual must work closely together. This may involve several people in the organization, but the key for the CFO is to assist the businesses or business in creating plans with stretch targets and actionable items with full involvement and buy-in from the businesses[20].

The CFO leads the team in investing in businesses which will achieve the entity's growth targets and at the same time look for optimal costs of capital to finance those growth plans. As in many places in this book, the value-creator CFO's ability to bring in capital markets' perspectives is imperative. The CFO can help the enterprise see itself as the seller of value, "selling future cashflows of the enterprise" (seller of shares – if the stock is traded on the stock market). And when one is selling a company's shares – something unique, given each company's unique attributes, one can set the price. If you think of the stock market as an auction, the seller can still set the reservation price. Therefore, the value-creator CFO, bringing in this perspective, can help the enterprise to align its own valuation to the market's.

The CFO's role is a very important role as success for the company hinges on it (financial strategy flows out directly from the corporate strategy). Without a value-creator CFO who

---

20 To the business leaders, some of this may sound like things that they are already taking care of. I recall in my "CFO" job at DTE Energy Distribution, working under Bob Buckler, president of the group, one of the directors in the operations once told me during a value creation session: "You are preaching to the choir." To which I quickly retorted that "the choir needs to hear the sermon every now and then, lest they fall into temptation."

knows how to formulate and deploy these strategies, the company can be stuck in "good" but will never be "great." I am being generous here. A mediocre CFO will be on the scene while the company is "slouching towards Gomorrah."[21] The changes must be valuable to last, because financial engineering or window dressing in the company's financials can only be temporary. While luck may be preferred, à *la Reagan*, skill will go a long way for the company to create value. This is why an entity needs to select a skilled CFO, it can make a lot of difference. Everybody can be a CEO, but not everyone can be a CFO, as the role comes with the need for specialized knowledge, such as understanding of the capital markets. Hence, the CFO should bring the necessary finance and strategy skills to the table and partner with the CEO to help the organization create value.

To create value, the strategy has to go beyond how best to compete and which businesses the organization should be in. The strategy should also define the role of corporate control – in other words, how business units will be measured from the corporate center. This allows the CFO to argue for how best to spend the organizational capital. This is applicable even in a not-for-profit environment. The CFO needs to lay out the business case to convince the executive team of the need to allocate resources to better-return businesses. In the same way, the value-creator CFO can "call the play" and exit from businesses which are draining corporate resources.

The CFO must be an advocate for deploying resources to the best-run operations, in order to increase the value of the

---

21 The words made famous by Judge Robert Bork when he did a play on words on W.B Yeats' poem – "The Second Coming" and made it his book title.

enterprise and shed non-performing assets or operations. The CFO needs to have presence and gravitas to be able to manage the overall executive relationships to achieve the corporate control objective. The terrain should be navigated carefully in order not to repel those who can formulate better businesses later on. The value-creator CFO must be in the position to frame the need for value creation and articulate the same to the leadership team. This needs an environment where dialogue is encouraged. Servant leadership traits will work better here. Specifically, empathy and listening will come in handy for the team. In essence, the value-creator CFO should be a negotiator *par excellence*.

In a nutshell, the CFO facilitates with the team to set in motion the purpose of the organization, the processes to be followed, and help develop the people who will help create value in the organization.

The CFO then helps to develop what I call the price-tag on that strategy or purpose and puts in place key performance measures (or targets) as well—in other words, what it will cost to perform the mission of the entity, the return on that cost, and how the organization will know if it is on track or needs course-correction.

The CFO is responsible for the financial books of the company. The financial books help the company in financial reporting for external and internal purposes. This should incorporate tracking processes and management reporting packages up to the board level so that the organization can keep track when implementation of the actionable items from the strategy begins. All CFOs maintain financial books for the enterprise.

The books are the measurement systems of the company. The companies' main books include:

1. Income Statement — which reports revenues, expenses, gains, losses and net income
2. Balance Sheet — a snapshot of the company's assets, liabilities and capital at a point in time; and
3. Statement of Cashflows — reports the sources and uses of cash for the company.

These three "books" or financials help answer three important questions for all entities:

1. What return is the entity making? (Income Statement)
2. What are the risks in the entity? (Balance Sheet)
3. Does the entity have sufficient cash? (Statement of Cashflows)

This is where information technology comes in. And as can be imagined, knowledge in technology can lead to tremendous value creation. It is recommended for the organization to have a dynamic and integrated financial system which has the capability to incorporate all reporting metrics, including operational data, for accountability and accuracy to occur. Better decisions are made with such "all-knowing" information. The CFO "resides" at both the gateway of and exit of data for the company.

Now more than ever, the CFO needs to be knowledgeable in Information Technology to lead the team, even if they have a strong IT group, as Finance must play a critical role in digitizing all finance and finance-related functions that lend themselves easily to automation. Here I am addressing specific functions in general accounting, cash management, accounts payable, accounts receivable, and the like. For the value-creator CFO, these areas can make a big difference. The list above constitutes what is referred to as working-capital items. Efficient management of working capital can help boost the company's returns. It requires a methodical approach, as the details are important. In fact, sometimes I have had daily reviews on cash to make sure that the required actions are being taken or executed with regards to cash management. The CFO would like to make sure that the company is taking every discount it can get and paying on time, not before, to preserve cash, enjoying the float, to achieve the requisite return for the company. The CFO needs to train the staff and share the same passion of working through the working capital with the needed diligence, after all, it is all about cash. Technology is the best enabler here, as timely information is needed when managing working capital.

Freeing up time in these areas, using Artificial Intelligence (AI) and algorithms, will allow the CFO group to embark on proving the data used to formulate insightful value-creation ideas for the business to work on. The CFO organization can play the feedback and feedforward role to identify areas for value creation for the organization. This will also allow Finance to respond in a timely manner to pressing value-creation initiatives across the organization and also to act as a strong clearing house for information, to improve operations. A good example here will be when I have worked with the timekeeping system for the organization to get an idea, in advance, how much overtime the organization has already recorded before the period closes. Sometimes, Operations want to know how much they are spending on a specific initiative, in order to decide whether to continue or terminate a program. Finance's ability to have this information readily available will go a long way in helping the value-creation effort. As the controller of the DTE Energy Nuclear group, using the existing information systems, I designed programs to get a good idea of how much the group had spent of their budget and what they had already committed, and using the run rate, adjusted spending targets or froze spending in some instances to avoid the mindset of spending the budget before year-end.

In addition to ensuring that there are adequate controls to safeguard all assets (both physical and intangible), the CFO is responsible for all financial reporting and compliance with applicable laws and regulations. To create value is to preserve value already created. That is why the value-creator CFO focuses on ensuring that a strong internal controls team is part of their group. I have personal experience in this area, as I have resurrected two internal control departments in my career[22]

As I mentioned earlier, I come from a public-accounting background, so I have an inherent control-based background. In fact, I wrote an article[23] in 1999, which provided an input into the Sarbanes Oxley Act[24]. I believe that the value-creator CFO is continuously looking into controls and using the

---

22 In his book *Conspiracy of Fools*, Kurt Eichenwald writes about the disregard of the internal controls at Enron, and of course, the tacit approval from the public accounting firm, leading to a corporate and financial scandal of epic proportions.

23 Excerpts of the article appeared in the August 1999 edition of the CFO magazine, as a letter to the editor, where I argued that there was a need for strong controls and better corporate governance to prevent a financial meltdown.

24 I shared the article with the Securities & Exchange Commission back in 1999.

Sarbanes-Oxley requirements to improve the business. It has been said that complying with Sarbanes-Oxley has increased complexity and costs. The value-creator CFO knows how to use the data collected, as part of Sarbanes-Oxley compliance, to create value[25].

Where will the resources to run the business to achieve the company's objectives come from? This is usually shown in the budget or plan, an outgrowth of the planning process. Organizations sometimes separate budgets into two: operating and financial budgets. The operating budget is used in controlling operations, whereas the financial budget reflects the financial decisions of the firm and is reported to owners of the firm.

As mentioned previously, to create value, the company must have a higher return than the cost of money (referred to as cost of capital) used in the business. This is where cash comes in, as cash is the ultimate arbiter in assessing whether the company is growing profitably or not. It is also applicable to the not-for-profit organization. Will the not-for-profit entity be around to serve the needs of its stakeholders? This is a pertinent question here as well; it will depend on how resources are being managed.

While companies have to report their financial statements

---

25 During my tenure at DTE Energy, I led the Fixed Assets group to comply with Sarbanes-Oxley. While the data collection of assets to be unitized was onerous, unitizing assets is important as it gives a clue into the quality of future assets to earn income for the entity. Unitizing is the process of closing completed projects and putting them on the books as fixed assets. I recommend that management make a review of that process as part of its monthly financial reviews. Future earnings depend on it.

using Generally Accepted Accounting Principles (GAAP)[26] — depending on the jurisdiction wherein it operates, the value of the company is better assessed based on cashflows. Hence, managers should look beyond accounting to understand the cash impacts of their decisions.

You have probably heard it said before that "cash is king." Well, in that case, the CFO should know the king very well, because regardless of the form of entity that has employed you, having cash on hand and having enough cashflows will be the main job of the CFO. It would be a good idea to ask the CFO at your next cascade or townhall meeting how the company is doing on cash.

Speaking of cascade or townhall meetings, I am of the belief that employees need to know the company's strategy and its tactics to achieve that strategy, all the time. Given that belief, I have always held a townhall meeting in my CFO departments (with the focus on leadership and learning), everywhere I have been a CFO. I recommend it. As part of the townhall meetings, I take the team through the company's strategy, financial targets, and concrete plans to achieve the targets. There is a team-building part also, to ensure that the team is connected as a group aiming to achieve the same purpose.

When I was writing this book, I took a break one day to go to the Costco in Sacramento, CA. I ran into two of my former colleagues from CalPERS at the food court on their way out, after shopping. After we exchanged pleasantries, I

---

26 US GAAP has statutory or regulation authority, unlike those of other countries such as the United Kingdom's. Companies can run into trouble not following the US GAAP.

asked why they were there shopping at Costco. They said: "We came to buy items for the townhall tomorrow." Knowing that I had passed the Fr. Cunningham test[27], I exclaimed: "I guess I left you all something." As the CFO, I introduced the CFO Townhall at CalPERS and led the first one.

The CFO should always keep an eye on the cash, as it is coming in and going out! While there are several role descriptions for the CFO, in general the CFO's role is to be in charge of the organization's resources: plan, obtain, and manage them. This includes reporting, controlling, and safeguarding those resources.

Most entities have to report externally every year. In the USA, publicly traded companies have to file quarterly and annual reports, and any material development with the Securities & Exchange Commission (SEC). Material information, in this case, is any information that has the potential to impact the value of the shares of the company.

The SEC reporting follows a format approved by the Commission, and the accounting follows GAAP as promulgated by the Financial Accounting Standards Board (FASB). The accounting numbers do not always agree with the cash measure of the company, at least on the surface. This is why it is important for the company to use cash to measure its success, as value is based on cash and not necessarily on accounting numbers.

Not-for-profit entities also report annually, as required

---

27 In their book *Every Business Is a Growth Business*, Ram Charan and Noel Tichy state on page 314 that Fr. Cunningham, the charismatic founder of Focus: HOPE in Detroit used to say: "Don't put my name on a building or boulevard, make my work live on."

by various regulators or associations. Public pension funds, for example, compile an annual financial statement among unaudited other data, as part of the Comprehensive Annual Financial Report (CAFR), encouraged by the Government Finance Officers Association.

Companies outside of the US follow the reporting requirements of where they publicly trade. The International Financial Reporting Standards (IFRS) is used for financial reporting performance around the globe.

Most financial statements have to be audited by accounting firms, usually referred to as public accounting firms. They render opinions on the controls of the entity and the financial statements emanating from those controls. Their opinions are usually qualified or unqualified (there are various degrees and exceptions, and even then, there is an instance where the auditor decides not to give an opinion). Most entities strive for unqualified opinions. That is to say, in general, that is the case where the public accounting firm does not find anything materially different from the accounting and auditing standards (while the accounting rules can be prescriptive, there is still room for interpretation). For the value-creator CFO, it is important that a public accounting firm known for its high-caliber[28] work is retained for this assignment. The entity cheats itself when it relies on sub-standard audit firms.

---

28 I tread carefully in this area, as some one-time high-flying public accounting firms have been known to have allowed certain practices, contrary to those allowed by the financial regulators. However, my standard for selecting an auditing firm is one where the collective knowledge and tools of the firm (their resources) must be perceived to be higher or better than those of the in-house management.

Today's CFO has to make sure that employees like yourself are fully developed for their tasks and have the right tools to get the job done. When the value-creator CFO is leading and framing the need for value creation, it becomes important that implementation or execution is flawless, and that is where a well-developed team is needed. Therefore, employee development, for the CFO, is not just development for the finance staff, but rather for the entire entity's staff, as developed employees help improve efficiency and create value.

The CFO works closely with the Human Resources (HR) department on this crucial element. I believe in this so much that I have helped HR departments develop leadership training for supervisors in companies. In fact, that is one of the reasons for this book. I believe it is important that everybody knows what is expected for the CFO to create value. Value is not created in a vacuum, but rather with informed and energized employees. Regardless of the nature of the entity, "The Cycle of Leadership" culture will create great leaders in the company who will teach others for the company to win and create value in their chosen fields. The value-creation CFO supports creating and maintaining an organization focused on culture[29] and on people development through coaching, mentoring, and personal development planning. Not to discount local nuisances, one global corporate culture for all geographies can be

---

29 As Louis Gerstner says in his book about his turnaround of IBM: "Who Says Elephants Can't Dance?" – Culture is everything, if the organization is to make a huge impact in value creation. By the way, I had the opportunity to speak with him about his turnaround at IBM in South Bend, IN, where he, a family friend, and President George W. Bush, among others, were receiving an honorary doctorate from Notre Dame. Louis Gerstner chose a tough and able CFO, Jerry York, to help him turnaround IBM.

created for the company in the USA, China, Mexico and all other areas where it operates. As the employees emerge in their career and personal development, those with leadership abilities must be encouraged and given the appropriate exposure to develop their business acumen. The high potentials with leadership abilities must be encouraged to answer the call of leadership. In other words, current leadership should foster an environment which engenders interest in leadership in the organization.

The value-creator CFO advocates for an organization where decision-making follows a rigorous process. My experience in business, however, tells me that executives make decisions based on analysis, and sometimes with gut instinct as well[30]. However, it is better that there is a rigorous process in the company for employees to follow. As stated elsewhere in this book, that is one of the legacies of the Whiz Kids at Ford Motor Company. It is very easy for companies to resort to a haphazard way of making decisions, for many reasons – expediency probably being at the top of the list. For an organization to create value, it is important that a consistent and uniform approach is in place, often referred to as the operating system. Later in this book, we will discuss General Electric (GE)'s operating system – an annual integrated business and leadership process (made famous by its legendary CEO, Jack Welch). Knowledge in Six Sigma tells us that variation in processes

---

30 Once the CEO of Palabora and I flew overnight to London from Johannesburg with some investment bankers from South Africa working on a deal with us. During the discussion that morning, the lead banker said that "her gut…told her…." My CEO, who probably had a sleepless night on the flight from Johannesburg, couldn't help himself. He blurted out:" We are not paying you for your gut instinct…."

(including decision-making) can be a big problem for a company when it comes to improving its performance. Ensuring consistency in processes is important also for entities for whom safety is a major issue[31]. Consultants like McKinsey, Accenture, and the like are sometimes pilloried for their "theoretical approach" to solving business problems. However, I find their approaches very useful. They have helped organizations that I have worked for to create some consistent processes. In fact, the value-creator CFO is a consultant at heart. That CFO wants to make sure that the organization has a consistent process to follow, especially in routine matters[31]. I have worked with McKinsey consultants in the past to deliver value for some organizations.

Speaking of HR, the CFO needs to be part of the benefits and compensation discussion so as to create incentives—for example, bonuses—which are aligned to the performance expectations of the company.

I remember that at one place I worked, the annual budget that was developed prior to my arrival had no input into the bonuses. As mentioned before, the strategy, processes, and people are related and work better in an organization when they are linked together. Goals and their measurements work better when tightly linked to incentives.

After the CFO has worked on the strategy and ensured that

---

31 You would be amazed what focus on quality can do for a company. It has been stated that the 72nd Secretary of the United States Treasury, Paul O'Neill, put tremendous focus on employee safety while at Alcoa, where valuation of the company increased from $3 billion in 1986 to $27.53 billion in 2000. He is known to have used principles of the Toyota Production System, where process control is a backbone of that system.

a proper business plan and budget are in place, they then help the organization to execute its mandate in the most efficient manner. That applies to the CFO and their department as well. The CFO then begins to keep score.

You have probably heard about Key Performance Indicators (KPI). The CFO works with other leaders in the organization to set these targets, including the financial ones, to ensure that the organization stays on course to achieve its mission, as spelled out in its strategy, in the most efficient manner.

The KPIs have to be approved by the board as the board monitors management's performance to achieve the strategy approved for the entity. Some companies use the Balanced Scorecard to measure progress. The Balanced Scorecard focuses on four main areas to measure and monitor progress of the mission: Financial, Customer/Stakeholder, Internal Process, and Organizational Capacity (learning and growth).

As you can see, these measures can bring comprehensive co-ordination as the company focuses on growth, cash generation, and better margins. For example, a focus on customer service, as we have seen elsewhere in this book, can lead to better margins. The other important point about the Balanced Scorecard is that it helps the company to monitor its performance today and into the future, whereas many financial measures are only backward-looking. On the other hand, the Balanced Scorecard provides an insight into what the organization is doing today to create future shareholder value. While the value-creator CFOs operate in an Augmented Reality (AR)[32] world, as they

---

32 Augmented Reality (AR) occurs when digital information is superimposed on the physical world.

work toward a future already calculated, with advancement in technology and budget methods[33], the approach should be commonplace in the not-too-distant future. Every value-creator CFO should know the likely impact of every financial decision made in a simulated world. Some companies (especially in Europe) are using (or overlaying) on the performance measures what is referred to as the Triple Bottom Line (TBL); it measures the company's impact based on these three criteria as well – Social, Environmental, and Financial. As the Environmental, Social, and Governance (ESG) activism gains grounds in corporate management and investing, the TBL will become an inevitable measuring tool. The value-creator CFO supports ESG, given that whatever business one is in, it needs a sustainable environment and practices to continue.

Achieving results energizes the whole organization, and of course, it will become profitable for you as resources increase and bonuses and dividends are paid.

Again, after the strategy is set, the CFO goes about determining the price tag, which includes the exercise of determining how much in resources the organization will need to deliver its mandate and what it will get in return. This is an extensive endeavor. This is another area where the CFO plays a dynamic

---

33 I have argued in the past that companies annual budgeting should be "cash budgets" directly for each organization. In current practices, most organizations perform a cash budget on a global or total company basis, whereas I argue that it should be at the lowest level possible. I came up with this idea in the '90s when I was working at Ford Motor Company. I believe that since it is all about cash, it would allow all parties in the company to pay attention to how their activities affect cash one way or the other. I hope that with advances in Information Technology, cash budgets for departments and businesses will take off in the not-too-distant future.

and resourceful role, because the CFO needs to help the organization see where it is creating value, and if not, what actions to take to change the direction for the better. Depending on where you work, you may assist in setting the necessary targets for the mission or provide needed data to support the decision-making process.

These exercises of setting the "price tag" have different names, but the most common is the budget (the annual portion of the business plan). Every department puts together a budget every year or when the operations are starting out. As I mentioned before, this is the price tag for which resources are needed to accomplish the mission entrusted to the department. The exercises also capture the level of sales, the number of retirees to be served, or whatever the department's goal measurement is. Remember this is an outgrowth of the business plan, as the actions to be taken are outlined in the plan. Some executives prefer the Zero-Based Budgeting (ZBB) method, meaning that they like to start from scratch to see how best to run their operations. In other words, they hit the reset button. ZBB requires all costs to be justified with their expected benefits to the enterprise. This approach can be used to better align resources and people to initiatives with higher returns for the enterprise.

This is also the time that the CFO facilitates with the executive team to think about the future of the business as it relates to its growth and cash generation, leading to value creation.

Your department will have action items that it will perform to support the overall mission of the entity. Then, the items are costed out, depending on how many people (sometimes referred to as headcount or complement in the jargon) will be needed, what types of materials will be used, and other costs to get the job done. Some costs, such as travel and training, may be discretionary in nature (we will discuss this later) and can be modified accordingly to the level of production or engagement.

The sales and marketing team, working alongside the business development organization, will scan the marketplace (or competitive landscape, if there is competition) to get an idea of the level of sales that the market will bear or can support. The in-house production team will assess the feasibility of supporting those levels of sales. As you can see, there is a lot of dialogue that needs to take place to get a well-thought-out product or service.

If it is an industrial (production) entity, there are also the costs for investments (physical assets) for equipment or buildings which are referred to as capex (as previously encountered). The CFO leads these exercises in identifying the costs by working closely with the businesses[34]. The value-creator CFO spends a lot of time creating policies to bring about honest discussions, as the capex determines the future earnings and quality of future earnings for the entity.

After several iterations and interactions within the company and at various levels, the CFO usually goes in front of the board to get approval for the budget spending (after the CEO's blessing). Sometimes this will include both the operating and capital spending. In other instances, they are handled separately. Capital spending budget requests can lead to interesting

---

34 Of course, these exercises can be led by those deputized by the CFO as well.

and broad discussions at all levels in the company, especially at the board level.

Next, the CFO has to find a source to fund the price tag[35]. In the parlance of business, this will be called the capital structure implementation, or simply "fundraising." A company's capital structure usually includes three main sources: equity, borrowing or debt, and past profits that have been reinvested into the business (referred to as retained capital). The capital structure is usually decided in the start-up phase of the enterprise. Even if it has been in business for a long time, the capital structure is revisited as part of the planning process to ensure that it is efficient and corresponds with the type of business and its competitive landscape.

In the case where the entity has already been in business for some time, the sources will be different and probably well established, but again, the approved or proposed strategy will tell.

The CFO may have to borrow for the entity, in a form of issuing a bond or borrowing from a bank. Sometimes, equity is issued; other times, trade credit is also used to supplement the funding sources. Issuing equity is where the company sells a portion of itself to investors and uses the proceeds to finance itself.

Remember, the business is creating value when it is earning more money (higher returns) than it is paying to use these sources of funding (referred to as the cost of capital[36]).

---

35 The sequencing can be such that this step is performed or lined-up before the CFO goes to the board.

36 The cost of capital is the weighted average cost of the composition of sources of funding to the company. I have an interesting story here:

In not-for-profit entities, the funding to run the operations is appropriated by an agency responsible for the entity (it can come from fundraising or from an endowment, which is money set aside to be invested and used for a purpose). Sometimes, the funding is from the entity's own operations. In the case of CalPERS, the employers who sponsor CalPERS for their employees pay from their budgets, appropriated by the respective authorities, city councils, the California Legislature, etc. (on the pension side, the actuaries determine the cost for an employee's pension in the future and then bring the costs to today's dollars, considering inflation and the return from investments – this is the bill CalPERS sends to the employers and employees[37]). Don't forget that the employee also pays a part (or contributes towards their retirement) – the 13% we saw earlier in this book.

One of the most important things that the CFO should be thinking about always is the risks and opportunities that can affect the organization (we'll cover that in detail in Chapter 6).

Apart from the CEO, the only executive who really sees and knows all that goes on in the organization is the CFO[38] (and some-

---

when I was an MBA student in Ann Arbor, I was invited by Microsoft to interview on campus for a job. I was the last person on the list that day. The recruiter asked me how I would calculate the cost of capital for Microsoft. I took him through all the steps and at the end, he held out his hand. I was not sure what was going on, so I asked. And he said, "Shake my hand." So, as any True Blue would do, I did! And he told me that all day, I was the only person who was able to explain this to him correctly.

37 Technically, a bill is not sent to employees; employee contributions are deducted at source from their paychecks.

38 And sometimes, the CFO will be the only person who knows what is going on, given that most things boil down to dollars and cents.

times the Chief Operating Officer [COO]). However, the CFO is
in a unique position, as they have solid numbers and facts behind
every story or issue going on in the company.

In many ways, the CFO should be a jack of all trades, and in fact sometimes they can be master of some, as they must have superior knowledge in matters of finance and accounting. This knowledge is critical; you cannot ask a non-pilot to fly a plane. They should know how to set a strategy and implement it. They must be familiar with efficient processes and also be knowledge-able about the legal framework that they are operating within. During the research for this book, the notion that the CFO should be licensed just like a pilot came up. I am not sure if earning a CPA license would be enough as a value creator CFO should also be very conversant with capital markets and how value is created.

The story is told of the Goldman Sachs CFO David Viniar, who through his nudging, was able to help Goldman Sachs avoid the mortgage meltdown as part of the GFC (Great Financial Crisis) and even for Goldman Sachs to profit from it[39]. The CFO should always be on the lookout for issues that can negatively or positively affect the entity.

The role of the CFO has been described variously in different organizations. Here are some examples:

1. Co-pilot: Focusing on the lifeblood of any entity – cash – the CFO works closely with the CEO to ensure that the organization is run smoothly. CFOs must have complementary skills to ensure that ideas that CEOs

---

39 How Goldman Won Big on Mortgage Meltdown; A Team's Bearish Bets Netted Firm Billions; A Nudge From the CFO, WSJ, December 14, 2007

present have solid backing in facts and numbers. The CFO acts as a sounding board for the CEO and heads of the divisions of the company.

2. Magistrate: In some cases, the CFO will have to play the role of a magistrate to ensure that disputes between departments and or divisions are properly arbitrated. I played this role when I was the key analyst working at the Ford Motor Company's $5 billion engineering spending desk. In fact, in order to settle budget disputes, I created a budget transfer system, which helped facilitate something that had bedeviled the group prior to my arrival. The CFOs will also have to enforce discipline on spending or any actions to ensure that the organization functions as required. The CFO is also the one to help develop key performance measures for each business unit and help ensure that they are followed by the respective business unit.

3. Engineer: In some respects, the CFO is an engineer, as they must master the entity's processes and systems to ensure that they are run well and efficiently. The CFO can also be the architect of the business models that will assist the company in creating value, determining what works well for the entity and its mandate. The CFO must also be in a position to help the enterprise build the necessary skills for better execution.

4. Consigliere: The CFO must be calm and rational, as they are bound to go through many business cycles or political climates, be a trusted counsel in the executive ranks because they are normally logical individuals

based on their training and personality. They must also work on commanding the respect necessary to challenge key assumptions in the business plans and also provide the necessary benchmarks for value-creation. In essence, they must be knowledgeable in several disciplines (remember the word I used earlier – versatile).

5. Catalyst: The CFO, serving as the spark, is the one who encourages the team, as a coach, to allow all parts of the organization to work together to achieve its optimal performance. Of course, some of the CFO functions touch on the CEO's role; that is why it is important that there is alignment between the two and that the CFO has the necessary support and leverage to rally the troops in the executive ranks. To create value, it helps if the CFO plays both the coach and cheerleader roles, without relinquishing the mandate to hold others accountable when needed.

The CFO can be many things for the organization. They can be the storyteller, muse, and even the leader of the rescue service (depending on the CEO's personality, sometimes these latter roles are performed by the CEO or shared accordingly).

However, no matter the nature of the organization, to create value for shareholders and stakeholders, the CFO will continuously be looking into the following:

1. Auditing value-creation: In this exercise, the CFO continuously looks into the strategy of the organization to ensure alignment of the discrete parts of the organization to see where it is working as designed and looking into the processes to determine, for example, where

more revenue can be generated (new lines of business or increasing prices) or costs can be decreased, without sacrificing quality (they will assess all the levers of the business, levers being the items that move the business one way or the other). Mergers, acquisition, and divestitures have occurred from this exercise. If your CFO happens to hold the Chartered Financial Analyst (CFA) designation, chances are they know how commercial entities are valued by Wall Street, so they will look at the business from the capital markets perspective, to see if the valuation of the company is consistent with how the company is being valued by the Street (certainly they don't have to be a CFA charterholder to know this, but it helps). They focus on the Price-to-Earnings[40], P/E ratio – which is assigned to a company based on its future cash generation prospects, all things considered (or sometimes not, as some executives like to argue with the analysts). Indeed, this is one area where the CFO should take a leadership role, of course with the blessing of the CEO to ensure that the organization stays on track to meet its commitments or pinpoints areas for improvements to unlock the intrinsic value of the enterprise. In a LinkedIn post, I referred to this as "Demystifying the Earnings Call" and the point was for CFOs and their management teams to not lose focus of the earnings call which is to guide

---

40 The P/E ratio is the price of a share divided by the annual earnings per share. It represents the dollar amount an investor is willing to pay for one dollar of the company's earnings. A higher P/E ratio is desirable, as it shows that the capital markets have confidence in the future prospects of the company.

analysts to properly value the company. When I did my first Investor Presentation, I laid the ground for future communication, and on following communications with the investment community, I tried to take the analysts back to that day and "walk" from there or point to where the "walk" was changing from that "Ground Zero" moment. This indeed is what must happen on Earnings Calls, as each earnings report should refer back to the company's strategy so that analysts can follow the company's "walk" – where they are going and how they plan to get to the desired valuation.

Let me say a word on valuation here. The simple concept is that the value of any company (or asset), is the present value of all cashflows from the company, discounted at an appropriate discount rate. The stock market operates on cashflows. Therefore, it is important for CFOs to help outsiders see these future cashflows for the entity to be valued appropriately. Security analysts or investors make judgments on companies and industries based on the quality of earnings, the quality of management, and the cyclical nature of the industry. These items can lead to a discount or premium for a particular company when compared with an index or the broader market. An index is usually the value of a basket of companies in a specific sector or based on a set of criteria agreed upon. Hence, cashflow certainty into the future has a huge impact on a company's valuation.

2. Monitoring the performance measures: The CFO will be active in setting targets and working collaboratively with the other executives in the various departments

and business units to put focus on the entity's mission and ensure that it stays on track. The CFO will lead several performance reviews, at the executive committee level and ensuring that the board is up-to-date on the entity's performance. In essence, monitoring is a very key role for the CFO. This gives them an opportunity to rally the troops for course correction when necessary. A word on course correction—it is important that the CFO and team pay enormous attention to the various parts of both the corporate and financial strategies so as to anticipate to the best level possible (or stress-test the targets and assumptions) so that when the original numbers from the budget targets and assumptions miss their targets, they do not resort to knee-jerk reactions, which often lead to unnecessary lay-offs of employees. Planning well to execute well should be the CFO's mantra. Massive restructurings should be reserved for only unforeseeable events.

3. Creating robust financial reporting: In addition to keeping score, the CFO wants all stakeholders to have accurate information. It is also helpful for the CFO and team to develop concise reporting, as it helps surface issues that need correction. I believe that companies are effectively run when they communicate in a transparent fashion. To that end, I have created very readable and transparent annual financial statements. One way I have accomplished this is to involve several members of the team to read and comment on our financial statements before they are filed publicly. So, this is another area when people who are not directly

involved in finance, like writers, can help the company create value, as there is a premium for clear and concise reporting. There is a need for internal financial reporting as well, usually as part of management financial reporting. Having explained the need for matrix organizations, I believe that management reporting should not be a surprise to the operating management. It is, rather, a tool for management to understand where activities are taking place and costs being captured as a result of those activities. No wonder, some management financial reporting systems use Activity-Based Costing methods, among other methods. Activity-based costing analyzes the entity's activities to identify the drivers of costs incurred and what leads to inflection points, to make the costs increase or decrease.

SUMMARY

We learned that to create value, the CFO has to lead the process in setting a realistic corporate strategy, lead the financial strategy, put in place a strong system for budgeting and management control, and then provide the highest level of financial management. They also focus on people development, leading through learning, and setting compensation with HR to incentivize and motivate the employees. They also encourage a value-creation mindset in the organization to foster a culture of innovation and process improvements.

Ask Yourself

1. Can I articulate the main role of the CFO now?
2. Am I able to find my involvement in any of the CFO's functions to create value?
3. Am I interested in working to create value for my organization?
4. Have I developed a plan to get into the action of creating value for my company, whether at the front line or supporting role, whatever my function is in the organization?
5. Have I checked to find out what resources are available for me to develop myself to create value in my company?

— II —
WHAT THE CFO DOES

4

DEVELOPING THE PRICE TAG[41]

As DISCUSSED IN the previous chapter, the CFO's job is to put an annual price tag on the business strategy. That is an outcome of the financial strategy. In a more stable environment, such as a utility company, this exercise is usually done for a five-year period and refreshed annually, taking into account changes in economics – that is, changes in interest rates and inflation or general costs of doing business, including increases in salaries.

Of course, the price-tag label that I am using here is just a name for us to get comfortable with the idea. In fact, for commercial enterprises, a better name would be a Profit and

---

41 Famous quote: While writing this book, I took a break to read a Financial Times (FT) article called: "Dinner with the FT Emir of Kano." Following an FT tradition, the Emir said to the author: "You routinely include the price tag." When the FT interviews somebody over a meal, they usually include the price of the meal in the article – an itemized table. Well, here we are trying to include the price tag on creating value. Really, the CFO must quantify the expected value, every time a planning or budget exercise takes place. The Emir was once the Governor of the Nigerian Central Bank.

Loss (P&L) tag, as some businesses will end up with losses at the end of the financial period. Or better yet, the value tag, as this exercise should be done with a new value for the entity in mind, especially if it is a commercial enterprise. Granted, in the not-for-profit sector, the measurement unit may be different, but the idea of coming up with an incremental value through an integrated business and financial exercise remains the same, regardless of the profit motive or otherwise.

The exercise includes both revenues that the enterprise anticipates for the year, as well as the costs associated with achieving that level of revenue. I'll show you the various components using the Alphabet Group's 2017 financials (Alphabet is Google's parent company).

As stated by the founders, Larry Page and Sergey Brin, they started the unconventional company to make big bets to improve the lives of millions of people—an ambitious and far-reaching goal by any measure. So, if you are working at Google, I hope this helps you to see the part that you are playing in Larry's and Sergey's vision or objective.

Like all commercial companies, the CFO of Alphabet has to be cognizant of all the various avenues available for the company to earn money. The CFO of your company would like you to be aware of the various ways that your company makes money, as well. The value-creator CFO leads the team in seeing how the revenues and costs are related, in order to create value. I have seen organizations which merge, and as part of their "synergies," take out layers of employees immediately; sooner or later, the merged company fails. The management fails to see the interconnectivity between the revenue levers and the cost levers. The assumption that a reduction in cost will only lead to better bottom lines has presaged many companies into their failed business status.

You have probably heard the story of the 3M employee who came up with the idea of stick-it notes when singing in church[42] , needing a bookmark for his hymn book. When you are conversant with your company's business and mission, you can think of adjacencies which can end up becoming profitable for the company.

Adjacencies are areas which, at first glance, may seem unrelated to your business but upon closer inspection will be discovered to be closely related to the core business. An example would be Adidas entering the apparel business when shoes are its core business. Entering into such areas can lead to higher profitability for the company. You can also think of General Electric reaping additional revenues through leasing and financing. They financed airplanes, rail-cars, and trucks and made incremental financial income from the equipment they had manufactured.

Developing the price tag will include management pulling all levers of the business to ensure that it is meeting its obligation as mandated by the board. Let me talk a bit about for-profit businesses before talking about not-for-profit entities. The key distinction here is that for-profit entities have a revenue component, while most of the not-for-profits have only to contend with costs (or resources) to run the entity.

This is an area where partnership between finance and

42 3M is the Minnesota company formerly known as the Minnesota Mining and Manufacturing Corporation.

operations is of paramount importance. The operations people know the business very well, and when they dialogue with finance about the business, light bulbs can go off for both sides to identify areas for potential growth opportunities. The CFO will indeed appreciate all employees being aware of the ways that the company makes money. In all my CFO jobs, I have encouraged this type of dialogue.

CFOs focus on the drivers of the business that lead to margin advantages (improvements) and better returns on invested capital (ROIC).

Let's look at an example of how margin is calculated: Your company earned $10 million in one year. Its total costs in that year was $7 million. Therefore, the margin (or profit) from the business was:

Revenues – Total Costs (taxes included) = Margin

$10 million - $7 million = $3 million (or 30% profit = $3 million/$10 million).

If we assume the invested capital to be $15 million, this organization will have a ROIC of 20% ($3 million/$15 million).

Again, if we assume a cost of capital of 10%, this company will have excess returns of 10% (20%-10%). This is a good business. Remember that the cost of capital is how much it costs the company for the money used in running the business.

On the next page, there are formulas to help those who would like to calculate returns for their business. These ratios help the entity to determine where they are creating value.

PROFIT MARGIN
1. Gross Margin = Total Revenues – Direct Costs (Products)
2. Net Profit Margin = Total Revenues – All Costs

VELOCITY
1. Turnover of goods by frequency, i.e. the number of times you can sell the goods or services.

RETURN
1. Return on Assets (ROA) = Profit Margin x (Sales/Assets)
2. Return on Investment (ROI) = Profit Margin x (Sales/Investments)
3. Return on Equity (ROE) = Profit Margin x (Sales/Equity)
4. Return = Profit Margin x Velocity

EXPANDED VERSION
1. ROE = Net Income/Sales x Sales/Assets x Assets/Equity

Note: Sales and revenues can be used interchangeably.

Beyond the ratios here, the CFO has access to several other ratios which can be used to assess and manage the following:

1. Profitability—mostly on profit margins and return on capital
2. Efficiency—mostly on how well the entity is managing working capital
3. Liquidity—focuses on the entity's ability to meet its cash requirement

While these ratios are available for all entities to manage their businesses, I think everybody should know about the Acid Test! The Acid Test ratio is a quick way for the CFO to tell if there is enough "cash" or liquid assets[43] on hand to cover current liabilities. Hence, the ratio is referred to as "Quick Ratio" as well. It is calculated by taking current assets, subtracting inventory, and dividing the net balance by current liabilities. Anything over 1 is good; if less than 1 then, some inventory may have to be sold to cover all current liabilities, in a pickle.

So, in developing the price tag, the CFO leads the team to focus on ways to improve the drivers of the business. For your company, that may include opportunities or sources for growth, how can the company operate better, and what parts of the business model can be changed to bring improvements on either the top-line (revenues) or bottom-line (earnings). Every company is a growth business, if approached properly. Not only must the company be concerned about growth, it should also look into creating value. The point is that there is profitable growth and non-value-added growth. Non-value-added growth is growth for growth's sake, which can be costly.

The CFO leads the team in asking some very pertinent questions during this exercise such as:

---

43 No wonder the French call cash, "liquide" (pronounced "likid").

1. How much is our business worth on a cashflow basis?[44]
2. What will be the new value after considering the new initiatives (specific actions and strategies emanating from dialogues – a collective action with input from all relevant stakeholders) that the company is proposing for growing the business?

In this exercise, the CFO would like you to think of the core mission of the business. For a car company like Ford Motor Company, how many cars will it produce by year during the planning period, usually referred to as the Cycle Plan. How many iPhones Apple will produce for sale and what models?

The costs to produce the products at the current prices (of inputs – labor [including your compensation and benefits], material costs, etc.) will be determined and then the costs will have to be increased for economics—that is, inflation, foreign exchange effects, and then a mark-up—on the products to be produced. Here too, the CFO is concerned about increasing value, so any market share increase that the company plans to gain must be vetted properly to ensure that it is *profitable* growth.

One question any board must ask itself is: "Are we ready to meet the activist investor?" The activist shareholder is the one that buys into a company and tries to push management to improve its value by changing its strategy, focusing on certain parts of the business, or divesting entirely from certain lines of business. This is done with the goal of creating value.

---

44 This is one area where CFO expertise differentiates the company from the competition. The CFO should be able to work with the team to quantify the incremental cashflow accruing to the business from its new action items. This action well done, will eliminate knee-jerk short-term cost-cutting and restructuring which are common in the marketplace.

The point is that this should be part of the annual planning process. The CFO must play a significant role here, since he is "from" the corporate center and should look across the business to determine if business units are creating value, when all the strategies and actions are combined.

This is the time that the CFO, working with the leadership team, tries to answer the question: "Is the company creating value in its new plans or destroying value through its proposed actions? Is the leadership team managing the business by adding value through taking advantages of synergies? Does the leadership team have the best financial acumen in-house to focus on cash or value creation?" The CFO also tries to work with the leadership team to create vision for areas which can generate revenues and better returns for the company.

In my past jobs, I have created "mini" CFOs to help the businesses create value. Finance needs to be there when decisions are being contemplated to provide a value-added counsel to ensure that the company creates value in the process. As the CFO of CalPERS, after my initial strategic review of the operations, I thought that it was imperative that we had a mini-CFO for the healthcare side of the house, a $9-billion annual spending business. I believe that a finance lens into the healthcare operations would have led to some significant savings or strategies to reduce the quantum of the spending.

To illustrate, we'll take a look at the 2017 Income Statement of the Alphabet Company (as shown in Fig 4). It's the CFO's job to ensure that all cylinders of the business are being fired to generate the maximum revenues. In a sense, the CFO plays the role of leading the leaders. In companies where there is a COO, the CFO will work hand in hand or be "joined at the hip" with the COO to achieve this goal. The CFO will be asking the following questions:

1. What are the value drivers of the business?
2. What are the key risks and opportunities?
3. How does the business compare with the benchmarks or the competition?
4. Have we pinned down specific business plan initiatives to create value?

As in the case of Alphabet, the company's subsidiaries such as Google and Other Bets, which includes all "baby subsidiaries" like Waymo – its autonomous driving division, are in the business of taking bold bets, with more future focus.

In 2017, Alphabet (mostly Google) made its money (approximately $111 billion) from advertising – performance and brand. Performance advertising allowed users to interact directly with companies from ads created and delivered by Google. In brand advertising, Google helped the companies to deliver digital videos and other types of ads tailored to specific audiences.

During the budgeting or planning phase, the CFO team, working with the marketing and sales department (usually there are better results if all affected groups in the company are involved) will ensure that all the levers of these sources are accounted for – in this case, how many users will be online using the internet and from which platforms, Android or Apple (iOS). One major item that the CFO focuses on is price; at what price point will the company be able to sell its products or deliver its services? It calculates its break-even point price, the price at which it is able to meet its costs. Again, as stated earlier, this is one of the areas where investment in technology and people can yield substantial results.

In addition, the CFO has to provide an objective or realistic view of the assumptions underlying the planning or budgeting exercise. They will have to consider the historic growth patterns and anticipated total companies' spending on advertising and even by geography, taking into account the competition or how these types of revenues may grow or decrease during the upcoming year for the various risks factors that affect the company's earnings potential. This is important, as unrealistic forecasts to be reduced drastically later during the year may have disastrous consequences for the company.

Next, the CFO will have to work with the entire team to determine the costs to achieve this level of revenue. These costs will include personnel cost, such as salaries, bonuses, and benefits paid to employees (in 2017, Alphabet incurred $46 billion in Cost of Revenues).

In addition, there are material costs, expenses paid to suppliers and contractors, and discretionary spending. Some of these costs will be deemed direct costs, meaning costs directly associated with the production of these revenues. Others will be indirect costs. These costs are not directly related to the level of production.

Discretionary spending is the costs for items that are not directly tied to the mission or the business at hand. For example, costs for attending conferences can be deemed discretionary spending.

Alphabet's 2017 costs included research and development, sales and marketing, general and administrative, and European Commission fine. I am sure that your company's costs are similar to Google's (maybe not, especially the one on the European Commission Fine!).

FIG 4

Alphabet Inc.
CONSOLIDATED STATEMENTS OF INCOME
(In millions,)
Year Ended December 31,

	2015	2016	2017
Revenues	$ 74,989	$ 90,272	$ 110,855
Costs and expenses:			
Cost of revenues	28,164	35,138	45,583
Research and development	12,282	13,948	16,625
Sales and marketing	9,047	10,485	12,893
General and administrative	6,136	6,985	6,872
European Commission fine	0	0	2,736
Total costs and expenses	55,629	66,556	84,709
Income from operations	19,360	23,716	26,146
Other income (expense)	291	434	1,047
Provision for income taxes	3,303	4,672	14,531
Net income	$ 16,348	$ 19,478	$ 12,662

Source: Alphabet 2017 Form 10-K SEC Filing; Author Format

Costs are sometimes labelled as period expenses or capital expenses. The period expenses are those that the accounting rules require to be accounted as expenses for that period. In other words, they do not affect any period other than the current reporting period.

Accountants are known for their tit-for-tat ways of looking at things. This comes out of what we call the "matching principle." The matching principle states that costs in a period to achieve a certain revenue should be reported in that period (or accounted for in that period).

On the other hand, the capital expenses, such as the costs for a building or machinery are those expenses which will affect multiple periods. They are usually shown on the balance sheet as an asset.

Only the portion affecting the current period shows up in the income statement. So, for example, when the company buys equipment to be used in production, over several periods, only the portion used in the current period operations will be included in the current income statement. Accountants have a fancy term called "depreciation," and there is a method for calculating it to ensure that it is realistic for the business. Therefore, depreciation is the cost of an asset used in the current period, which can be accumulated over a period of time. In your company, these will be the costs for items like the building and vehicles used in generating the current income.

Actually, the term—depreciation—is really how much the company should be setting aside to replace the equipment or fixed asset when its time runs out. If you recall, I mentioned that the value of a company depends on cashflows, and yet the accounting is not directly related to cashflows. And that is because accounting for businesses uses what is called the accrual method or a modified version. The accrual accounting method records revenues and expenses when earned and incurred respectively, regardless of when cash is exchanged. Non-profit entities mostly use the cash method, where the accounting directly follows the cashflows.

The other major item which needs mentioning is taxes. Alphabet set aside $3.3 billion in 2017 for taxes. Companies usually do not pay these taxes directly – as they have certain deductions that they can take within a certain period of time.

In business, the term to pay attention to is called the effective tax – this is the actual tax amount that the company pays to the tax authorities, based on its effective tax rate. That is the normal or nominal tax rate adjusted for any deductions the company is entitled to take. To help in understanding this concept, think of the Schedule As and Bs that you fill out with your personal income tax returns. Companies are allowed to take deductions and adjust their incomes just as individuals.

In the not-for-profit entities, such as CalPERS, the price tag is usually the budget for the fiscal year (with some projections for the out years). Note that the fiscal year for governments and some not-for-profits entities usually runs from July 1st to June 30th of the following year. In this case, the price tag consists of costs for the entity to meet its financial obligations or achieve its mission. Again, the items in the costs will include personnel costs, materials and supplies, and discretionary spending items. What is missing here is profit, as these organizations are not in the business of making profit. However, they will show either a deficit or surplus if they receive less or more income respectively from their revenue sources.

Although they are not profit-making entities, the CFOs of these organizations usually emphasize efficiency. In other words, the CFO will establish targets for the entity to achieve. This starts by the leadership team agreeing on KPIs (Key Performance Indicators) and determining how each department would contribute to achieving those targets.

Back to the Alphabet illustration, the CFO then leads the team to determine the sources of cash and uses of cash. This leads to the statement of cashflows (a similar exercise is done by not-for-profit organizations as well).

The statement of cashflows is divided into three sections; cashflow from operating activities, cashflow from investing activities, and cashflow from financing activities. Cashflows from the operating activities are from the actual business of the entity (when it comes to valuing companies, the quality of the cashflow here and its sustainability are very important).

As shown in Fig 5 below, Alphabet ended the year with a little over $37 billion in cash from operating activities.

Alphabet's
2017
Sources &
Uses of
Cash

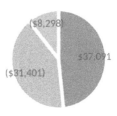

($8,298)

$37,091

($31,401)

• Operating Cashflow   • Investing Cashflows   • Financing Cashflows

Source: Alphabet 2017 Form 10-K SEC Filing, Author Format.

FIG 5

Source: Alphabet 2017 Form 10-K SEC Filing, Author Format.

Cashflow from investing activities – which is the net cash
the entity used to invest in the company or received from selling assets, which are not part of the normal operations of the
entity. From Fig 5, Alphabet ended 2017 "investing" $31 bil-
lion in the company that year. Investing in the company is
acquiring assets for the future use in producing income for the
company. Finally, cashflow from financing – which contains
the sources and uses of cash from and to investors, creditors,
and others associated with financing the business. In 2017,
Alphabet ended up spending a little over $8 billion with capital
providers to the company.

Before leaving the statement of cashflows, I would like to say a word about financing an entity. Entities (such as start-ups) source funding from friends and family, outside investors (beginning with Venture Capital Funds), and then creditors who lend funds to these businesses.

CFOs budget the sources of funding for the business each year as well. In fact, this is highly recommended, as it helps them to source the most efficient funds from the capital markets. Planning ahead is always helpful. As we say in business, the time to borrow is when you don't need the funds (as the cost of borrowing for an entity increases astronomically once the entity is in financial distress). Once again, value is created when the company earns more returns from its operations than what it pays for capital used in operating the business. The ability to source the least-expensive and most-efficient capital will be beneficial to the enterprise in its quest to create excess returns (or value). The CFO, working with the treasurer, must be scanning the capital markets for the least-expensive funds that can be raised to finance the business.

The normal finance theory advocates what is called the Pecking Order for sound capital structure management of the enterprise. The pecking order theory holds that companies should fund the business from internal funds first, and then borrow or issue debt but issue equity (or float shares) only when all options have been exhausted, as issuing shares can send the wrong message about the company's future prospects to the investing community. It can be a sign of overvaluation of the company in the stock market. Companies usually do not want to dilute their share prices if they believe that the company's future is brighter than the current stock price. That is why companies buy back shares when they think that their company's value is more than what the shares sell for in the stock market today.

Like some theories, the pecking order theory does not hold all the time, as there are technology firms for whom issuing shares leads to an efficient financing strategy than borrowing, as borrowing costs can be very high due to the inherent risks or volatility in the technology sector. Therefore, risky businesses are better off selling shares than borrowing, as they pay more to borrow than less risky businesses do.

The finance team then leads the exercise of creating a balance sheet, projecting what the assets and liabilities along with the ownership, and source of funding for the activities would be like at the end of the year (or period).

Let me remind you that the statements that we have discussed so far are all the results of an actual period. So, as we say in finance, these statements are ex-post (after the fact) as opposed to ex-ante (before). Internally, Alphabet would have a projected balance sheet, a roadmap, from its planning exercise, which the CFO would have consulted on a regular basis to see if the business was on track, in order to report to the board of directors and all stakeholders, as a publicly listed company. These planning statements are known as pro forma financial statements. Pro forma statements are also put together when companies are contemplating mergers and acquisitions(M&A). In other words, what would the combined companies look like after the proposed action?

Before we leave this section, let's answer the question as to how Alphabet is doing in using other people's money. As you will see in the data from GuruFocus.com below, Alphabet had return on invested capital (ROIC) of 28.43% versus an average cost of capital of 11.67%. In effect, it was earning excess return of approximately 17% — that is good business:

*As of **today** (11/3/2018), Alphabet Inc's weighted average cost of capital is **11.67%**. Alphabet Inc's ROIC % is **28.43%** (calculated using TTM income statement data). Alphabet Inc generates higher returns on investment than it costs the company to raise the capital needed for that investment. It is earning excess returns. A firm that expects to continue generating positive excess returns on new investments in the future will see its value increase as growth increases. (Source: GuruFocus.com – Date November 3, 2018).*

This exercise can produce several scenarios before management presents likely ones to the board. These scenarios must be stress-tested to ensure their ability to withstand changes in the marketplace. Stress-testing these budgets will assist the company to avoid the short-term reactions, commonplace with some companies due to the temporary vagaries of the marketplace. Stress-testing allows the company to gauge its performance under several conditions, especially during dire conditions.

After all this information has been compiled, the CFO, along with the executive team, presents this information to the board or sometimes to a subsection of the board before presenting to the plenary board for their approval. Each executive will have specific items for them to speak to from the business plan. Find out what your executive has committed to this year as part of the value-creation process in your company.

Usually this leads to a very robust discussion at the board

level. After all, the role of the board is to set or approve the strategy for the entity. One way of thinking of the board in relationship to the entity is that the board is like a rudder of a ship. It sets the direction that the ship must travel, with the CEO as the captain navigating the ship (the company) to shore with the CFO at their side, making sure that the journey is done in the most efficient manner with enough money to meet its commitments, including robust returns for shareholders. The plan or budget is just the "price tag" of the strategy approved by the board. In some instances, multiple versions or various scenarios are presented for the board to adopt one.

SUMMARY

The point I want to leave you with is that your CFO would like you to know that the activities we have described here occur during the budgeting or planning cycle. As mentioned previously, the strategy will have an impact on this exercise. The financial management of the company will also affect the budgeting or planning phase as well, as that system will provide the necessary data to inform this exercise. Financial projections are made for various items in the plan. These statements are usually referred to as the pro forma financial statements. The planning process, which is led by the CFO and staff, may involve everybody in the enterprise. It follows a cycle, so you can become comfortable with what is expected of you during the planning and budgeting period.

If you are not familiar with the timing of your company's planning cycle, ask somebody in the Financial, Planning & Analysis (FP&A) department in the CFO's office. Not only will this help you to prepare for requests from the CFO's office, but it can also help you plan your time away from the office to spend well-deserved time with family, doing continuing education, and the like, without jeopardizing your career or reputation in the work place. When the CFO's office begins to sing your praises about how diligent you are with your work, you can begin to go places.

Ask Yourself

1. Do I know my company's planning schedule?
2. What is my role in the planning process?

5

CFO MAINTENANCE

THE BUDGET OR financial plan has been adopted by the board. The entity now has a roadmap to a destination, a target, where it is heading. This is where financial brinksmanship comes into play and separates a good CFO from a mediocre one. There are many functions that a good CFO performs to ensure that the enterprise is run properly and that value is being created for shareholders and all stakeholders alike.

This is also where business acumen is needed, which is the knowledge to see things on a holistic basis and to encourage processes to be performed in a manner that helps the company in its competitive landscape. The CFO wants you to learn business acumen. It reduces stress as you learn to maneuver in complex situations; you will become comfortable in sorting through what needs to be done to achieve the organization's mission. The value-creator CFO is also creative and innovative as they possess a lot of knowledge about different subjects (versatile) and can bring them together to help the company win in the market place. Again, it is about linkages and the ability to balance the task at hand, helping the organization to reap better returns and finding reasonable lower costs of capital to operate.

We have learned that the CFO puts emphasis on the strategies and tactics that create value, including working for improved margins (profitability), generating more cash faster, and ensuring that the assets are generating better returns than the costs for funds used in acquiring those assets. To continue to create value, the emphasis is on doing this day in and day out. The CFO ensures that this discipline is pervasive in the company's culture.

In leading the team to create value, the CFO is continuously asking these questions:

1. Is our company growing? Growth comes in many forms. Sometimes, it is organic – which is in-house growth. Other times, growth occurs from M&A when the company combines with another entity.

You will remember that the question about growth prospects was asked (or should have been asked) and deliberated upon during the planning or budgeting phase (it is never-ending). To maintain the pace for the company, the CFO continuously pays attention to the growth question. This is done as actual data is reviewed during the year or period where the budget or plan is being lived out. As an employee, paying attention here can be good for your career, and understanding what is going on may help your development as well. Are you seeing trends that you can share with the financial leaders?

For example, a higher volume of customer returns of products can be an indicator of the company's future prospects, or lack thereof. The CFO needs to be aware of this type of information and work with the executive team to devise corrective actions.

Are the company's revenues growing or declining? Are the assets of the company in good shape? Here is one of my favorites: people in the maintenance department of the company may not realize the big role that they play in helping the company to create value. When the maintenance schedule is kept, and the assets are in good shape; downtime is minimized and production can occur at scheduled times befitting the company in turning assets to revenues as planned. So, on a regular basis the value-creator CFO is keeping an eye on this or has somebody in the CFO shop whose job it is to watch maintenance spending and schedules to ensure that the company is performing its scheduled maintenance. There is a higher cost to pay if equipment breaks down and there is no insurance in place, the company suffers from production disruption, and of course, the additional maintenance costs, not to mention liability to third parties from faulty assets. Again, you can see that creating value is indeed circular. And that is part of the business acumen, paying attention to actions or consequences from the company's operating or financial activities (or lack thereof)[45]. The CFO must continuously

---

45 During the writing of this book, Sacramento, CA was enveloped for about 3 days in smoke from the fire that burned down the city of Paradise, CA. PG&E, the northern California utility has been embroiled in a saga stemming from what has been termed as lack of maintenance of its equipment which appeared to be the cause of the fires, or at best a contributing factor to the disaster.

balance these actions to ensure that the company benefits from the renewed focus.

As you go through the planning process, you should be asking yourself these questions: How can your department help? Is growth cyclical or on a trend basis? Is it time to look for other opportunities outside of your company or industry? These are questions that you alone can answer but as CFOs ask themselves the question on a regular basis, you too must follow the trend to know what is happening in your company. Or perhaps, if there is a source of revenue that senior management is overlooking, now is your time to bring this up, especially if you interact with customers and hear what is coming on in the marketplace that can affect the future products or services of your company. The value-creator CFO also keeps up with trends to know when to advise the company to change course.

2. What are the margins from the company's revenues? It is also important that you are looking at the difference between what the company is earning, and how much it is costing for those revenues. This will tell you if the growth is profitable and where the company stands when compared with the competition.

3. Cash generation is also important, as any growth should be increasing cash (or have the potential to return more cash in short order), rather than depleting it. Therefore, in addition to wanting an increase in revenues, to be sustainable, cashflows from operations should be increasing as well. It is not enough to have more revenues, if those revenues are being generated on the back of giving away profits, and correspondingly, cash. For

example, when the sales department sells more at a discount (to increase their commissions, if incentives are not set properly) it is giving away future profits. This is also one of the reasons why the company KPIs or balanced scorecard should be all-encompassing, to ensure that everything is done to help the company achieve its overall goal, rather than serving the objectives of a few folks in the company, to the detriment of other stakeholders.

4. Return on assets – to maintain the well-being of the enterprise, the CFO, on an ongoing basis, is keeping track of the company's return on its assets. Remember that this return on assets is based on the company's margin and its velocity. Is the equity sweating? That is, is the company getting more bang for its money in generating better returns with a level of assets?

Communications – the CFO has an important role in communicating the enterprise's mission and strategies to achieve them to the investing community, employees, and all stakeholders. As part of the CFO's investor relations role, a detailed report of who owns shares of the company should be studied to understand their motives of shareholding in order to ensure that management is delivering to expectations. For example, if a majority of the shares is owned by funds or people who need regular income, then the maintenance of dividend payments or periodic buybacks should be part of management's balanced strategy to return funds to shareholders. Ignoring something as simple as that can have negative consequences on the company's share price. This is part of the linkages that I described earlier. In other words, the company could be investing for the long-term but if that is not balanced against the needs of current shareholders, the company could be missing the mark.

The CFOs of publicly listed companies perform annual reviews with investors (in some organizations, it is called the Investors' Day). CFOs of private entities, or governmental entities perform similar roles with their boards and other stakeholders. The CFO's team needs to track analyst views on the company's performance and prospects. The value-creator CFO takes time to listen to the analysts, debate ideas, and incorporate some market thinking into their in-house strategies and tactics. The market is a repository of information, and when tapped into properly, the CFO will be well tuned into managing value as well[46].

As stated previously, the CFO's staff also communicates the planning cycle to all employees. Such communications help with expectations and deliverables. In today's environment,

---

46 I have practiced this strategy and am here to tell you that it works around the globe. It worked for me in South Africa. You are probably thinking of what Ross Perot told Bill Clinton during their presidential debate when Clinton touted his achievements as governor of Arkansas. Ross Perot said that was like being the manager of a corner grocery store and thinking you could run Walmart. As it turned out, Clinton proved that if you can manage the corner grocery store well, you can manage not only Walmart, but the largest economy in the world – the United States of America! In many ways, Barack Obama has also borne testament to that truth; once you have the basics down, you don't need to be a governor or CEO before becoming president of the largest economy in the world. I dare not leave out Nelson Mandela. As I have learned, you pick up a lot of skills working in some of these international business circles, as I had the chance to work with people in Asia and Australia through my African experience. You can learn the basics well and apply them at scale when the opportunity arises and be very effective. In fact, in a smaller outfit, you get to do many valuable assignments earlier in your career than you would in a big shop.

most of this communication can be found on the company's website. I encourage you to look for that on your company's website, or the website of any entity that you are interested in following.

As a side note, several companies run on a December 31ˢᵗ financial closing schedule. For companies that are located in the southern hemisphere, the CFO has to make sure that employees are available to close the books in December as it is the summer season there and with children being out of school for the summer, maintaining a full complement can be challenging.

Publicly traded company CFOs follow up on Investors' Day communications with earnings calls on a quarterly basis. This is how they report earnings, where they review performances and guide the investment community about future financial projections. They also present at investment conferences.

Analysts who follow publicly traded companies build models, mostly using Discounted Cashflow (DCF) techniques to value the companies. As pointed out previously, companies are valued based on their cashflows and their ability to generate sustainable cashflows. The value of any commercial asset, company, or entity is just the present value of all cashflows, that is free-cashflow on hand (money left after meeting commitments).

To ensure alignment and understand how the investment community is valuing the company, CFOs and their teams build their own models to show how value can be created in the enterprise.

If you recall, when we discussed developing the price tag,

I mentioned that the CFO would like to develop a pro forma income statement, statement of cashflows, and a balance sheet, as part of the budgeting or planning exercise. These statements underpin the CFO's communications with the investment community. In a similar way, the statements are used in discussions with the board of trustees of not-for-profit entities as performances are monitored during the year.

When the CFOs communicate with investors, the CFOs try to guide them to the assumptions used for the company's own in-house financial statements (and valuations) so that the market valuation may not be far-off from the company's valuation. Of course, there are general factors to an industry or country that analysts factor into a company's valuation that a company may not necessarily consider in its own valuation. I have also mentioned that items such as the quality of earnings (how sustainable they are) and the quality of management also factor into an entity's valuation. These factors may explain a huge market premium or discount from the company's own valuation.

As previously stated, one of the key roles of the CFO is to lead this process of doing the in-house valuation of the entity and communicating with the investment community to ensure alignment. In other words, when it comes to value creation, the CFO has an important job of serving as a bridge between the company's valuation and the investment community's valuation of the entity.

When I was a student interviewing for jobs with public accounting firms for an auditor position, every company asked why I had majored in accounting and wanted to work for the

"Big 8," as they were referred to back then. They are now called the "Big 4" due to consolidations and the demise of Arthur Andersen, a casualty of the Enron scandal. The answer which I believe was parroted by almost every student was that "accounting was the language of business" and that working with the global accounting firms would enhance business fluency. In some ways, as I found out, public accounting did not disappoint, as I learned a lot in a very short period of time. What that explanation really means is that the finance organization touches every part of the business.

For those of you still in school and deciding on majors and want to be CFOs, public accounting should be one of the areas for you to consider, as it will help in your future career development. You can gain a lot of experience in a very short time. I was lucky to be pointed in this direction by the controller at Burroughs-Wellcome Pharmaceutical Company, when I did a summer internship in the controller's department.

A good CFO needs to be well-rounded, with ample knowledge about how the business runs, and knowing the linkages in the business to create value. Therefore, your CFO will advise you to get-well rounded experience in the company as well.

Sometimes, this is achieved by changing jobs. In addition, you may want to explore other opportunities, such as teaching at your local university, taking a graduate course, or enrolling in certification programs to enhance your overall knowledge and remain competitive in your chosen profession.

Good CFOs also know that industry experience does not matter as much as general business and finance experience—in other words, business acumen. I always find it interesting when companies advertise jobs looking for people from the same industry.

It may hold true that it is a better option to hire people with prior industry knowledge, but if the individuals have gone through professions such as public accounting, or possess an MBA or similar backgrounds, it does not matter. In fact, the case can be made that opting for people outside of the industry with appropriate technical finance background is better, as they bring "fresh eyes" to look at processes anew and can help the company achieve better results. I have had this experience on a personal level, as moving from industry to industry, I have been able to add value quickly in a new company based on the experience I had gained from my prior assignments in different industries.

I must add that the individual must be a quick learner who can easily come up to speed and become conversant with issues in the new industry[47].

To perform the role thoroughly, CFOs need a core team of finance people to assist them in the following areas:

1. Systems support to capture accurate records and protect data accordingly, especially finance records;

---

47 Charles Ellis, CFA of the "How to Win the Loser's Game" fame, a veteran in the pensions and asset management industry, gave me a nice compliment after my maiden presentation to the CalPERS Board of Trustees. A month after my arrival at CalPERS, I took the board through a presentation of asset liability management and the board's role in managing the same. After the presentation, Dr. Ellis walked up to me and said that my presentation was eloquent and that he thought that is how a good CFO could explain issues to the board. I had drawn upon my CFO experience in other industries in presenting to the board.

2. Accounting staff to perform general accounting functions such as payroll, posting journal entries, making adjusting entries, closing books; and

3. Cost accounting staff who will ensure that the costs to production or costs to achieve the mission of the enterprise are properly accounted for.

I cannot overemphasize the need for computer literacy. Earlier in my career, I learned some programming, which helped me to create programs for reporting, useful to management for monitoring and controlling. As we move more into AI, Analytics, and Big Data, it will continue to be profitable for you to be fully computer literate in your work. You'll improve your efficiency. The company is perched for tremendous value creation, if it is able to translate data into real-time insights for decision makers in the enterprise.

As it has been stated before, if the organization is going to be efficient to create value, it starts with the CFO organization. This is where the value-creator CFO uses tools from the Lean production or other such systems to eliminate waste and become efficient. When I first became the controller of the Fermi Nuclear Plant, as part of DTE Energy Finance group, I met with all my direct reports to list all financial reports that the finance group was producing for both internal and external use to the "customers" of the Nuclear Generation Group. Understanding the purpose of each report led us to recommend reports to eliminate. I put on my linkages hat and tried to understand how together those reports helped or did not help the enterprise to create value. In fact, some of them did not have any relevance to what the organization was trying to achieve. I then went to the corporate financial and operating leadership teams to get their consensus, as I explained to them that by eliminating the reports which were not needed, there would be tremendous savings all around. In the end, I was able to eliminate about 50% of these legacy reports, which were no longer creating any value.

The CFO also needs a strong finance team to assist in areas of corporate finance analyses such as whether to buy or lease equipment and to assess merger and acquisition targets and their potential benefits to the enterprise. As mentioned previously, growth can sometimes come in the form of a merger. In identifying a target and analyzing potential benefits, the group can benefit from a talented CFO team.

A strong tax accounting staff is also needed to ensure that the company pays its taxes but no more than legally required. The CFO also needs an internal control team and risk management as well. Proper ethics guidance should be developed and followed in the company. I have played a significant role here in various companies, ensuring that we had robust ethics guidelines in place. Be careful, though, as you can become a threat easily when you try to stop employees from malfeasance. In one company, an executive told me to watch the "Godfather" movie.

When a company is creating value, it needs to preserve what it has created already. Risk management will make it easy for the CFO team to keep an eye on the opportunities being taken and items that could put the company at risk if proper attention is not paid. Risk management is part of value creation. To achieve a return, a risk is taken. Value is created when the expected return is better than the risk being taken, or else the risk is not worth taking. The risk return ratio has to be positive.

To achieve its mission, the CFO will check continuously to see that the company is structured properly to serve the mission of the organization. To give the company value for its money, the CFO needs to benchmark its costs against peers to see how the organization can serve the company better. To that end, developing the CFO team is one of the top priorities for the value-creator CFO.

As mentioned previously, the CFO is usually interested in developing efficient, well-rounded employees. To run the company to meet both operating targets and financial targets, there is a certain discipline that should become commonplace in the organization. The CFO usually works with HR on this mission[48]. The areas for the organization to focus on to create such discipline include the following:

1. Technical system: Here the organization must put in place a technical operating system which applies standardized best practices. And it does not have to be from the same industry. Mining companies can take best practices from the aerospace companies, and vice versa. Some companies have adopted the Lean Manufacturing[49] or production method as

---

48 I started the "Finance for Nonfinance Managers" seminar at the Fermi Nuclear Plant; which became the harbinger of the "Learning and Leading" program at DTE Energy in Detroit. I later taught a course on leadership in the program [Positive Leadership], that was offered to all DTE Energy managers, including first-line supervisors.

49 The term is attributed to my former colleague, John Krafcik, now CEO of Waymo, as appeared in his 1988 article: "Triumph of the Lean

their standard form of operating – an efficient system meant to save money and enhance quality. Companies like Toyota, Alcoa, and Sandvik are known to have successfully used these methods in the past to create value. The CFO team needs an operating system to be effective.

2. Capability/Learning building system: I cannot over-emphasize the need for a learning system enough. The value-creator CFO leads the charge to make sure that the organization has standardized problem-solving tools (this can include Six Sigma, Kaizen, and others). Having used these tools in my former workplaces, I know that they work, and in fact, they help in building the value-creation mindset that the CFO wants to promulgate in the organization. This aspect includes initiatives such as the townhall meetings that I have described elsewhere in the book, or some type of an internal training for all employees or leaders.

3. Culture alignment system: As the leaders of the organization begin to embrace the value-creation mindset, there must be actions put in place to propel this culture. One area which stands out and can be a great motivator is if some meritocracy model is put in place so that people who perform superbly are awarded promotions or incentives, as that would bring in a competitive spirit and drive the process forward for the organization. The organization also needs to decide the type of talent—both quality and quantity – it would need and capabilities of its employees or potential hires.

Production System." I was on the Transit 2000 Refresh team with JFK (as we called him then) when we both worked at Ford Motor Company.

4. Performance management system: This is where the rubber meets the road. Is there a system in place to hold people accountable for not achieving targets? The system does not have to be punitive. So, for example, is there an After-Action Review process in place (AAR)[50], to help the organization learn what went well and what didn't, so that it can reap a better execution next time or share best practices with others in the organization? Does everybody know what the value-drivers are for the organization? The performance management system can include some type of feedback and feedforward system to help improve performance.

The CFO maintenance, as we have seen, is the process of making sure that there is a "software" in place to enhance value creation. That software would include enablers as well.

The CFO wants all employees to be familiar with the company's strategy and have the skills to support the company in its mission of value creation. If you are unclear about the mission, ask your supervisor. Find out how your company makes money and be able to articulate that when people ask you. Beyond that, the CFO wants all employees to be stewards and safeguards of the assets and resources of the enterprise.

---

50 As is commonplace in all branches of the US Military.

SUMMARY

The items necessary for value creation boil down to engaged employees, with all the necessary tools and processes thought out for creating value. The remarkable thing here is that several of these actions are being performed in the industry or marketplace and can be easily benchmarked.

Even if your company is a not-for-profit entity, knowing how your company gets its resources to operate (makes its money) will be important for your career as you learn to utilize resources efficiently. There is a premium for that – and it will set you apart from your cohorts.

Ask Yourself

1. Do I know how my company gets resources to operate?
2. Do I have the skills to contribute as well as I would like?
3. Do I have a plan to help contribute to the fullest extent of my ability?

6

Risks and Opportunities Management

As mentioned previously when we discussed the CFO's maintenance function, one of the key jobs that the CFO has is to constantly monitor the environment that the entity is operating in, to be aware of risks and opportunities that can affect the operations of the entity. If you recall, we learned earlier in this book that the first thing that the CFO focuses on is the strategy of the entity. Understanding the strategy means becoming familiar with the several levers of the business which can change within a short period of time without warning. Levers can be defined as specific initiatives or items that are directly associated with the profitability of the firm. An example is the sales volume. A company stands to create value if the volume of profitable sales goes up, whereas the value declines with decrease in the volume of sales. Also, there are various risks and opportunities that business units or division may face; the CFO has to consolidate all those items to determine the overall impact on the entity, and work with the executive team to take the proper actions to achieve the desired outcome.

These risk elements include changes in economics – interest rates, inflation, and foreign exchange impacts. Other risks include life cycle inflections, factor costs, global competition, regulation, and changes in technology. Economists refer to risks as either exogenous or endogenous.

Exogenous risks are those that will come from the outside, while endogenous risks are those originating from inside the entity. We spoke about risks and opportunities when developing the price tag. The CFO usually keeps a list of the known elements which can affect the planning numbers that went into the pro-forma financial statements developed as part of the planning process. The value-creator CFO ensures that this is thoroughly done, in order to avoid the recurring cost-cutting exercises that are common with value destruction. The organization must think ahead and stress-test its planning so that it does not give in to short-term cost-cutting, but embraces only the restructuring needed to change direction to position the organization for the long-term growth. This approach will afford the entity the temerity to follow its strategy, as opposed to giving into short-termism. Short-termism is the notion that companies manage on a short-term basis, to appease the stock market, while destroying value in the process. On the other hand, if the organization must cut costs, in order to align with market expectations at a point in time, this must take place expeditiously and be properly communicated. It will allow the company to avoid the spiral that some companies get themselves into, once the market begins to clamor for cuts and management keeps dragging their feet.

To create value, your CFO is continuously rethinking the company's strategy of value creation, as new information becomes available. First, we know that due to technology and global competition, the life span of any enterprise can shorten much quicker today than it ever did. Life cycles of companies have reduced tremendously.

Some of you may remember Sun Microsystems, or IBM for that matter. Not too long ago, these companies were heavyweights in the networking and computer ecosystem respectively. They have both pivoted to other areas as competition has forced them to rethink their business strategies. The CFO will do well to scan the competitive environment to make sure that the enterprise is heading in the right direction, and if not, to recommend the necessary adjustments.

We talked about capital investments. That is where the company spends money on physical assets which will yield more revenue in the future or sometimes just to maintain current level of business, as referred to as stay-in-business capital spending. On an ongoing basis, the CFO is relooking at the capital expenditure, as reports come in regarding the projected costs against approved spending. These reports are reviewed with other executives for course correction or to glean for better trends to follow to enhance the business.

It is imperative that somebody in the company ensures that spending will yield the improvements envisaged at the planning stage. The company will be better off, knowing when the inflection point has been reached and that pivoting into a different sector will be in the company's best interest. The CFO leads the team in figuring out whether the business is at an inflection point where capital spending should be reapportioned properly, as opposed to spending on infrastructure or systems no longer relevant to the company's core business.

Think of all the companies that Amazon has replaced through its strategy. First on that list is Sears, once an American darling and the world's largest retailer. Its parent company, Sears Holding Corporation (SHLD) declared bankruptcy on October 15th 2018.

The Economist, the British weekly magazine, minced no words, when it called Sears "once the Amazon of its day." Let's review the statistics when Sears entered into bankruptcy: Its stock market value had declined from $30 billion in 2007 to $69 million on October 17th 2018, with debts of almost $5 billion. Revenues were down to $16.7 billion in 2017, compared with $50.7 billion in 2007, and it had not been profitable since 2010.[51]

Naturally, the question that comes up is what was Sears management doing during this period? Did it underestimate the threat from Amazon? Was management unable to set up an aggressive strategy to defend itself and even go on the offensive with Amazon? By now, I am sure that you are getting the gist of what a CFO needs to do to preserve and or create value. Your CFO should be involved in analyzing the moves of the competition, especially from upstarts like Amazon entering its competitive landscape, to come up with strategies to defend itself.

A company's ability to generate superior revenues or profits goes beyond the physical assets (the brick and mortar). It

---

51 Tears for Sears, The Economist Magazine, 20th October, 2018

hinges on culture, people, and processes. Hence, the reason why a CFO should be involved in creating an atmosphere to offer the entity the opportunity to create the most value.

Perhaps the CFOs of retail companies displaced or being displaced by Amazon should have fought a little harder – worked with their CEOs to understand the landscape and what could happen to them. It is said that for Amazon's first fifteen years in business, traditional retail CEOs dismissed Amazon's encroachment by saying that e-commerce was just a small part of retail.[52]

If you have used Amazon's services, you know how good they are at customer service. The point is that in business, unless you are paying attention to all the factors of value creation as shown in this book, sooner or later, you'll have to give up your throne to a "pretender." That is what management calls them when they first appear on the scene.

The Economist, not one to leave a "dead horse" alone, had this to say about Sears' management's hope to restore Sears' fortunes: "Soon all that may remain of Sears are copies of its old catalogues, on sale on Amazon for $1.88."[53] The usual refrain from company executives about inability to compete is the cry about the increasing costs of factors of production.

We have come across the factors of production in some form or another before in this book, but probably now is the time to state what they are: the costs of the labor, land, capital and entrepreneurship, which are used in the production process.

---

52 The Four, the hidden DNA of Amazon, Apple, Facebook, and Google. Scott Galloway. 2017

53 Tears for Sears, The Economist, 20th October, 2018

One of the things that the CFO is supposed to do during the planning and budgeting processes is to work with the team to identify the optimal combination at the best prices (in the most efficient manner).

For example, if the rent cost for buildings (space) is high for the company, it should look into moving into a low-rent district. Sometimes, it can even sell its buildings in an expensive location for more money and move into a low-rent location. The point is that management, led by the CFO, should be continuously monitoring for opportunities to lower production or service costs, without sacrificing quality.

The CFO knows that to create value, there are various assets which are not necessarily captured in the company's financial records but must be harnessed. You will recall that we say that people costs, like your salary and benefits, are all considered as expenses. In many ways, you may be worth more (your value to the company) than those expenses captured annually and presented on the financial statements. The value-creator CFO will understand how the company must harness the skills inherent in the company to create more value. You have probably seen or come across this perpetual joke on LinkedIn:

CFO: What happens if we train them and they leave?

CEO: What happens if we don't and they stay?

It should just be that, a joke, because the value-creator CFO does not think that at all. In fact, as stated here in many forms, they are the ones that lead the charge to ensure that employees are well trained and prepared for their jobs. The value-creator CFO sees employee development as an investment to boost company performance.

The work of the value creation CFO is to assist the team to capture the intangibles that are not necessarily on the balance sheet. You may recall that I said the CFO's job includes ensuring that the employees are well trained to execute the company's mission. The real value in employees is how they make decisions, the quality of those decisions, and how they execute mandates given to them. There is more: How do the company's employees present the company in the marketplace? Do they have excellent relationships with both suppliers and customers? The value-creation CFO gets involved in the human side of the company in order to create an environment with a value- creation mindset. A learning organization also pushes the envelope when it comes to value creation. A learning organization is fertile ground for innovation and creativity, which can lead to profitable growth for the company through introduction of new products and services.

The CFO is interested in customer satisfaction because it is an indicator of how the company is creating value. In a similar manner, excellent supplier relationships can point the employees to opportunities including discounts on purchases and other business areas that the company can pursue later (think of adjacencies here also). Are there alternative uses of the company's assets that the employees, or through their relationships, can think of to bring additional revenues to the company?

When it comes to factors of production, the risks and opportunities are endless. The CFO and team must constantly be looking at what is happening internally and gather intelligence about what the competition is doing so that they can take appropriate actions to preserve the company's value-creation momentum.

The company stands to reap incremental profits, if it is the first to institute a policy that helps, for example giving part-time employees company-sponsored healthcare. This will reduce employee turnover and the attendant employee satisfaction will help in customer satisfaction, as satisfied employees are wont to pass along that intangible benefit (better attitude from the healthcare benefit received) to customers. This will lead to repeat business, and the reduction in employee turnover will also reduce employee costs. Recruiting and training costs will go down as well. There will be benefits all around.

The CFO must have superior knowledge to help the company when it comes to "economics" items like interest rates and foreign exchange. There are many instruments on the financial markets to help manage risks and opportunities in this area.

When I started my CFO job in South Africa, the company had entered into swaps (derivative instruments) with some banks in London, as part of borrowing from them. While it is easy to critique anything in hindsight and appear to be a seer, I believe that the transaction could have been structured a little differently, giving the company and even the bankers the chance to reset the agreement if market conditions changed. After all, a hedge is just supposed to be for protection, just like insurance. It should not introduce additional complexity.

With my background in derivatives, I was able to work with then Lehman Brothers in New York and London[54]. I took

---

54 Prof Dufey generously provided me very useful counsel on the derivatives issue.

two solid derivatives courses during my MBA studies and one of my derivatives professors worked at Lehman at the time[55]. We worked on a proposal for the creditor banks, Royal Bank of Scotland and Barclays[56], all in London, to understand the risks inherent in the new demands that the banks were making on the company when it appeared that the company might not be able to pay for the loan and the swaps. We showed our willingness to transact with others if they kept up the punitive measures. While the company did not have a formal credit rating, we were able to demonstrate that the risk profile had improved since the inception of the loan. We showed that the banks had some responsibility in the structures put in place, as part of the loan agreements. I found it interesting that during the Global Financial Crisis, the then President of France, Nicolas Sarkozy, was making similar arguments with the financial institutions about bailouts of European banks.

In a LinkedIn article I wrote a few years ago, I argued that the CFO must pick a capital structure that fits the profile of their business.[57] As we have been saying, creating value de-

---

55 For one of the classes, we used this textbook by John C. Hull: *Options, Futures, And Other Derivative Securities*. It was a pleasure to say hello to Prof. Hull in November of 2017 when I went to the University of Toronto Rothman School of Business to attend a board seminar. Prof. Hull was updating the textbook on the same day, believe it or not! I had studied the book on my own when I interned at the Dow Chemical Company during the summer between first year and second year of my MBA studies at Ross, to do a Put-Option study for the Dow Chemical Treasurer.

56 Barclays was also acting on their own behalf and that of ABSA of South Africa as well.

57 Charles Asubonten, Overhauling the Mining Capital Structure, LinkedIn, February 22, 2016

pends on the cost of capital that the CFO can find for the organization. The cheaper the better, the more commensurate of the type of business, the best.

In that article, I argued that every company has a risk component embedded in the volatility of the business; therefore, the capital structure should align with this volatility to complement the servicing of the cost of capital (both debt and equity). In other words, if the business is very volatile, or cyclical, debt-servicing must be at the level that the company can afford even in down cycles, so that the company does not go into bankruptcy. Bankruptcy occurs when debt-servicing comes due and the entity cannot afford the payments. While the company owes a duty to shareholders to create value, creditors can assert more pressure on a company in a distressed position.

SUMMARY

By their very nature, all organizations are subject to various risks and opportunities. The value-creator CFO works with the leadership team to identify these risks and opportunities. To create value or preserve value, the CFO monitors them routinely and strives to devise various tools to achieve desired outcomes.

Ask Yourself

1. What are the risks and opportunities that my company face?

2. How often do I hear the CFO talking about risks and opportunities facing the company?

3. Can I think of a risk that my company is not addressing?

4. Are there any opportunities out there that my company could be taking to create more value?

— III —
KNOW YOUR PART

7

HOW THE CFO IMPACTS YOUR DEPARTMENT

THE MAIN POINT to keep in mind about the role of the CFO is that the CFO is the guardian of the money of the entity. Of course, that is the simplest way I can put it. It is more complicated than that, as we have learned already. This cash is for all stakeholders. Everybody flourishes when there is enough of it to go around. Shareholders are handsomely rewarded when there is more cash than what it took to get the business going. Employees get the resources they need, and they are compensated for their efforts as well. Even the government gets in the act, as a well-performing company pays its taxes[58]. And in most jurisdictions, the company, or the board of directors, owe a duty to the shareholders to ensure that best efforts are used to preserve value.

---

58 When we reported some excellent set of financial results, my office got a call from the South Africa Revenue Service (SARS) to find out when we were paying our interim taxes. They sure did not want to be left out.

The CFO will impact your organization through the allocation process. As mentioned already, the role of the CFO is to ensure that the organization has the necessary resources to achieve its mission. In that respect, your department will provide information to the CFO's group. It is therefore important to understand the requirements so that you can accurately provide the information needed and your department, in turn, will receive the necessary resources to assist the CFO in the value-creation efforts.

One of the indicators of CFOs who create value is that they like to operate in a matrixed organization. In the matrix organization, there are finance personnel who report to operations as well as to the finance hierarchy. The matrix organization creates mini-CFOs for the different divisions or businesses of the company. The mini-CFO may be called by different titles in your organization, but the function will be to report to the CFO directly, and indirectly to the operations office. This allows the overall CFO to avoid command and control. In other words, you will find a person, from the CFO's organization, embedded in your department. This allows finance to be involved in the decision making earlier on and also to provide the necessary analytical support. The mini-CFOs become clear lines of communication between the divisions of the company and the CFO's office. They demystify the job of the CFO to operations as they pass information from the CFO to operations and vice versa. Your department will be sharing data and information with the CFO's office. When the CFO's office is a central depository of information, it allows for a centralized analysis which can be profitable for the entity. What all this means is that if you are not in the finance organization, you will have a liaison with whom you should work closely.

The value-creator CFO puts in place a process for all employees to be schooled in business acumen. You have probably heard of the "Whiz Kids." The Whiz Kids were a group of military veterans who after World War II joined Harvard University. They had used statistical and mathematical modeling to help in the war effort. When they heard that Henry Ford II (HF II) was struggling with Ford Motor Company, they wrote and told him that they were willing to bring their expertise, all of them or nothing, to help turn around the company. HF II accepted their offer and they subsequently joined Ford. Many of them rose to become executives of Ford, but the lasting legacy they left was a way of doing business. They left a manual of business acumen which has been used over the years. That is one way that the CFO may impact your department. The CFO helps the company build an "operating system," a way of doing business. Having such a primer helps create uniformity and infuse a particular way of doing business into an organization's DNA.

There are those of you who will be directly impacted by the CFO's work as you work in the areas identified as falling under the CFO's remit. And then there are those in other departments who may not work directly with the CFO but whose work nonetheless benefits the company's value-creation efforts.

So, for example, if you work in the strategy department of the company, you will help the CFO figure out what the competition is planning to do. Of course, as I stated earlier, to create value, the CFO has to worry beyond the competition to create an environment where the company is reaping the best returns, given its resources or looking for opportunities to leverage the entity's resources for better returns. Knowing the competitive landscape will assist in decision-making at the entity.

SUMMARY

It should be clear by now that a good CFO is a sine qua non for value creation. This individual becomes the coordinator, or the catalyst between the executive leadership team and the rest of the company on efforts to create value. They lead and then they serve to ensure that the people in the company have the necessary resources, skills, and tools to get their work done; and that the company has a solid blueprint and template in place to create value.

Ask Yourself

1. Have I participated in a budget meeting of my company?
2. Did I find it useful, or what would I change about it, if I had the opportunity to make changes?
3. Are my organization's rewards and recognition systems tied to value-creation metrics?

8

HOW TO SUPPORT THE CFO

I HOPE BY now you have become familiar with what the CFO needs, to create value in your organization. So, when you hear of these initiatives or requests from the CFO group, you will be willing to support them. Everybody benefits from a company which is creating value.

As stated earlier in this book, CFOs affect every department in all enterprises. The key for your development is to find out how the CFO impacts your department and support them accordingly.

I believe that armed with this knowledge, you will be able to take part in value-creation at your company. Depending on where you work, you may be directly involved in supporting the CFO. Wherever you work, your work has an impact on the company and its overall value-creation efforts.

To prepare yourself to be part of the value-creation efforts in your company, you want to make sure that you have all the necessary training for your job and that you are fully attuned to what you need to do to play your part to make sure that your enterprise is successful. The value-creator CFO works with HR to ensure that the organization has the necessary courses in the organization for employees.[59]

The value-creator CFO will be well supported, if you begin to own your career. Take inventory of your performance and see how you are supporting the value-creation efforts. If there are gaps, make sure that you and your supervisor have a plan in place to close that gap. One thing I have liked about my experience is that various companies give you opportunities to develop. I remember at my first CFO townhall at CalPERS, I asked by show of hands how many in the audience had had a listening course. Not too many hands went up. I told the group that that would be something for the team to work on. I had my listening course at Dow Chemical in Midland. It has served me well, as I have learned not to speak all the time, which is the natural inclination for many people when in conversations with others. As you are supporting the CFO and ensuring that you are working well with other members of the team, it will be to your advantage to take these courses, which are offered to improve one's effectiveness. In fact, these days many such

---

59 This is another core belief of mine. I remember writing a corporate strategy paper in the late Prof. C K Prahalad's class, where I argued that companies should even create their own MBA programs, to fit their strategies and unique circumstances. He really liked it. C K is the strategy guru known for the term "Core Competencies." In fact, I was part of the group at Ford who helped the company recruit undergraduates to be sponsored for their MBA program to be completed while they were employed at Ford simultaneously. The idea was for Ford to supplement what the employees would be learning from the MBA programs while they were working at Ford.

opportunities abound for free for anybody to improve their skills to become a valued member of the value-creation team. I can think of courses on Lynda.com, edX.com, and many others which will provide opportunities to improve your skills.

Teamwork — One thing that I have observed about companies that create value is that teamwork is encouraged in many forms. The value-creator CFO likes the organization to work together. In fact, if you recall, I said it is better if the organization is structured around the matrix model. Hence co-location is important, where different parts of the business will have access to each other to discuss ideas which can lead to more growth and more productivity. Join a group in your organization that brings people from different parts of the company to work on projects to improve the bottom line.

Technology — As I mentioned before, technology has given us many opportunities to improve productivity. The value-creator CFO is technologically adept and can use technology to automate many basic functions in the CFO's organization. Likewise, the use of technology in your department will help improve productivity as well. Learn more about technology and keep up as society evolves. Social media can also be used to improve one's knowledge through networking. Because of LinkedIn, it is now possible to reach a global group of people to seek opinions about any work issue.

SUMMARY

Three things you can do to support the value-creator CFO: Make sure that you have taken all the training your organization offers, learn to work in a team by getting involved in a team, and make sure that your technology skills are updated as society evolves.

Ask Yourself

1. Have I performed a career checkup lately?
2. Are my skills aligned with the direction of the company and its value creation efforts?
3. At this point, am I directly or indirectly involved in value creation in the company?

9

TIMELINESS

TIME IS OF the essence in the CFO's role. There are not many roles where time management is more important than the CFO's role. The CFO has to strike when the time is right. You have heard it said before: Time is money. After all, that is what the CFO's role is about – money.

The first thing the CFO works on is the strategy of the enterprise. This exercise leads to a better outcome when all relevant stakeholders get the opportunity to express their views. It is always a good idea for the organization to have several brainstorming sessions. This strategy should consider the views of all, including customers, suppliers, employers, community leaders, and all who could possibly be affected. As mentioned before, the CFO will ensure that investors' views are represented as well. Another key element for the value-creator CFO is information. You have heard it said before that during President Bill Clinton's first presidential campaign, as reported by the former Secretary of the Treasury, Bob Rubin, that the campaign was all about: "It's the economy, stupid."[60] It can be safely said that "Value creation is all about timing, stupid." The book of Ecclesiastes has already laid out the need for timing of everything. A time to sow and a time to reap. In a likewise manner, the value-creator CFO needs to ensure that the timing is adhered to for the organization to reap bountiful harvest.

Many organizations have timelines that they follow to create value. Let's look at an organization which was legendary for following a timetable for its success: General Electric (GE).

Under Jack Welch, GE held what was referred to as Session C in April and May. During Session C, corporate executives with the head of HR went to the businesses to do business reviews, focusing on the initiatives agreed from the prior year operating plan. During these sessions, people and their careers were discussed and debated. In fact, Jack Welch has called these sessions as brawls, gossipy, and brutally honest[61]. The organization's value-creation prowess depends on its people and their abilities. There is also the need to ensure that the right people have been put into the right jobs, and when that is not working, it is imperative for the executives to ensure that correction is made as soon as possible. The value-creator CFO is very interested in this process, as they know that the success of the organization depends on it.

Following Session C, the necessary people changes from the discussions in April and May would be made in July. There are organizations which take forever to make people changes.

---

60 As reported in Bob Rubin's book: "In an Uncertain World: Tough Choices from Wall Street to Washington"

61 Jack Welch said that in his book *Jack: Straight from the Gut.*

We saw that giving employees broad experience is also important for value creation. Hence, having a timetable that compels executives to make timely people changes enhances the value creation process. GE then did strategy reviews in June and July (referred to as Session I in GE parlance). Again, as said before, the value-creation process is circular. As you can see the business reviews conducted in April and May are now feeding into strategies for the near future. Strategy immersion sessions lead to a common understanding among all executives. Also, they are able to discuss the people in the organization who can help execute the strategies emanating from these sessions.

In October, Jack would hold what could be considered a townhall in my parlance, bringing together all officers of the company to lay out the broad themes coming out of the strategy and people meetings. And then in November, the business leaders would present their operating plans for the upcoming year (referred to as Sessions II and CII). The CFO plays an important role, in many of these instances — being the conduit between the executive leadership team (what is referred to as Exco in some countries) and the various businesses and functional areas.

It has been said before that the CFO organization presents the company with a timeline that will impact all facets of the business. From my experience as the CFO, I have been the guardian of these schedules and sessions. GE used the outcomes from these processes and meetings to communicate with investors[62]. In other words, when Jack Welch and his CFO spoke with investors, they had all the relevant information

---

62 As the CFO of Palabora, I used this approach in my communications with investors as well.

to guide the analysts with the analysts' valuation models of GE (recall I said this is a tag team between the CEO and CFO when it came down to ensuring that the company and the Street were on the same level). GE had other management reviews as well, they had what they referred to as Session D, focusing on compliance – an important facet given the necessity to focus on risk management, as part of the financial discipline. Indeed, time is of the essence when it comes to value creation. The CFO will make sure that a timeline has been laid out and that everything has been put in its place for that timeline to be met. In fact, as we used to do at the Ford Product Strategy Office, to make sure that submissions are met on time; we put in some slack, knowing that there are time differences among the various entities in the group, such as Ford Hiroshima, Ford Australia, and Ford Brazil. I am pleased to report that we always met our submissions deadline. The value-creator CFO knows that time is money and is keen to ensure that submissions are made on time.

SUMMARY

To create value, the organization needs a timeline which must be adhered to; the CFO leads this effort, and ensures that the process allows for feedback and feedforward for the strategy, people, and processes.

Ask Yourself

1. Are you familiar with your organization's value-creation timeline?
2. Is there a schedule in your organization allowing for mass job changes to enhance employee capabilities?

IV

GOOD FOR EVERYBODY

10

THE CFO, PEOPLE DEVELOPMENT, AND YOUR PERSONAL GOALS

BY NOW, I hope that you are very clear on the role of the CFO and how your work feeds into the CFO's value-creation efforts. As I have tried to show in this book, every part of the organization is needed to perform at an optimal level for value to be created in the entity. The CFO knows that the people of the organization hold the keys to excellent execution and robust results.

If you recall, I have said many times that the value-creator CFO's agenda includes making sure that the company has employees properly trained in their fields and are given the proper tools to perform their respective roles.

The good news is that when your CFO is a value-creator, your company will have many opportunities for your personal development. This starts with goal-setting, as part of performance management. You have probably heard it said before that you need to take control of your career or manage your career. Therefore, when given the chance, make sure that your goals feed into the value-creation efforts of the company. There may not be a direct link, but remember what I said before; every role in the organization is connected to the overall purpose of that organization.

Your CFO would have worked with HR by now to ensure that the requisite training for your role is available in the organization. In your own personal development agenda, you may reach for the necessary self-development books on business acumen and leadership to supplement.[63] As you read these books, pay attention to the CFO's role, as it is all-encompassing. As I said before, the value-creator CFO works with all parts of the business in the balancing act to create value.

So, for example, if you work at the customer service department of your company; as stated before, the interaction with customers is important for future and repeat business. Make sure that it is clear what customers expect and that working with your leadership team, there is a clear roadmap for you to achieve good customer relationships. By this, you will be supporting the value-creator CFO.

Once your goals are set, take time to go through the necessary training. This is important for both leaders and non-leaders alike. Depending on where you are in the organization, you may want to ask for some type of coaching, with emphasis on value creation, especially on business acumen. Try to

---

63 I'll recommend reading the books in the reference section at the back of this book.

understand the role of finance and basics of finance or value creation in your company.

While learning and getting to know your business, it is also important that you know what goes on in the organization other than your own department. This knowledge equips you to find opportunities where you can contribute more toward the value-creation efforts.

At this point, you would have probably caught on that this is not that difficult. Why isn't every entity creating value? Well, like all human affairs, it is a little complicated because sometimes there are leaders who pretend they know, when in fact they don't really know how to create value. The organization can be a little complicated, bullies abound. They rise to high levels, without the necessary skills, as certainly they have skills in politicking. My favorite example is the erstwhile Enron CFO, who according to Kurt Eichenwald, the author of *Conspiracy of Fools*, had no idea how to create value and yet maneuvered his way into the CFO position. And knowing how to play the corporate game, he made himself so powerful that even the Chair of the Audit Committee had apprehension approaching him.

There is also the problem of those who have believed in their own press so much so that they forget what it takes to create value. It would be helpful if companies would hire those who have the real knowledge, regardless of race or gender, and acknowledge that people are different and give those people the opportunity to perform[64]. When I was at DTE Energy, I had

---

64 I would like to recognize Alan Greenspan for giving minorities and women chances for leadership roles when he was at the Federal Reserve

lunch with an executive vice president who had met with Ram Charan the previous day. He went on to say how beautiful this world was, how you could find someone like Ram (an Indian from India), myself (a black man), and the president of one of the businesses at DTE Energy (a white guy – the same person who patted me on the back during the DTE executive strategy session I referred to earlier in the book), all very knowledge-able about business and yet with such diverse backgrounds, not least where we had been born[65]. I might have echoed this former DTE Energy Executive Vice President earlier when I wrote that nobody is an island. Knowledge seems to have been spread equally around the world. There are smart people from everywhere. And then there are some, of whom the late President Richard Nixon once said: "In a democracy, fools have to be represented too." The value-creation CFO needs to ensure that those people are not overrepresented in their entity, or worse yet, allowed to conspire, as they can utterly destroy value. Jack Welch once said that the operating system for run-ning the company needs to be such that any fool can run the company. I wonder what Jack thinks now about that, given what has happened to GE since his retirement. Elsewhere, I have written that CFOs should be members of their company's

---

Bank (USA). He wrote in his book *The Age of Turbulence* about how minorities are often overlooked and yet are very hardworking. Speaking of women at his economics firm, Townsend-Greenspan, he said: "The men worked for the women." I think the Maestro deserves a lot of credit here, even if he did that for economic reasons. His deputies at the Fed included Roger Ferguson, now CEO of TIAA/CREF, and Alice Rivlin, now a senior fellow at the Brookings Institution.

65 I have always wondered if the person with the key to eradicating cancer is not languishing somewhere in South East Asia or Africa. After Elon Musk (born in South Africa), the notion is probably not that far-fetched.

Board of Directors (especially in USA since it is already the case in Europe, Africa and some other jurisdictions) so that there can be continuity when the CEO moves on.

Once I attended a budget presentation at a DTE Energy St. Claire Shores plant. After the various presentations were made, the operating director in charge said something that has stayed with me: He said planning and working for successes in business is like "doing the hokey pokey – that's what it's all about!" The value-creator CFO leads the team to focus on the business, to have a solid strategy, ensure that the basics (financial management, budgets, etc.,) are right, and give people the tools and skills they need to do their best; day in and day out. It requires daily plodding and continuously doing so, or the "hokey-pokey." It's repetitive and circular but that is how value is created.

To close, I'll urge you to take an interest in value creation in your enterprise. If you are the CFO, now is the acceptable time to create the environment in your company that can get people focused and energized to create tremendous value. Wherever you work, your job supports the CFO in creating value. Take advantage of the various opportunities to develop your business acumen and execute your role flawlessly as you go back to your job with this renewed vim.

Epilogue

I HOPE THAT this journey was worthwhile for you. And that you have learned one or two things about the CFO's role and will be able to use them in your company to create value.

The ideas discussed in this book may sound simplistic, but I am here to tell you that the process to create value requires a lot of effort to make these ideas work. The ideas and actions must be linked to the overall mission of the company. Often, companies fail to create value because they ignore the simple things. A good CFO knows that you cannot leave the value-creation work to chance.

The one last piece of advice that I would give here is what is said about the price of liberty – eternal vigilance. In the same way, to continue to create value for your organization, the CFO must be eternally vigilant about being intimately involved in the corporate strategy, leading the financial strategy, ensuring sound budgeting and management control processes, and providing the highest level of financial management, as we have described in this book. That eternal vigilance applies to everybody in the organization, in the company's quest to create value.

As I bring this book to a close, I am constantly reminded of what has happened to General Electric, after Jack Welch. Tremendous value has been lost since Jack's departure. It all goes to show that we can't take value creation for granted. Jack had said that he was building a company that "any fool could run," but as it turned out, it wasn't that simple. This reinforces the notion that we should constantly give employees the opportunity to develop and hire people with "fire in the belly," as Lee Iacocca would say, to succeed us. You want people who are hungry for opportunities to create value, rather than those expecting the opportunity to be handed to them on a silver platter. Let's remember that our pension is dependent on how well the company performs in the future.

Every entity needs a CFO who knows how to create value and can bring the executive team together, with the backing of a CEO who knows the value of a good CFO. The CFO leads this effort being the "eyes and ears" on the company's ability to have enough money to meet all its commitments.

With our work cut out for us, let's begin anew and create value for all stakeholders!

About the Author

CHARLES ASUBONTEN

MR. ASUBONTEN, a serial CFO and strategist, has held top leadership positions in several sectors across many geographies and has a global track record of value creation. Presently, he serves as the CEO of Capital Hill Ventures, a firm which helps entities to build and sustain value.

He was one of the minds behind the turnaround of Palabora Mining Company in South Africa, then a publicly traded company on the Johannesburg Stock Exchange and a subsidiary of the Anglo-Australian mining giant, Rio Tinto. He most recently served as the CFO of CalPERS, the largest pension system and the second highest healthcare purchaser in the USA.

Mr. Asubonten studied business (at the graduate level specializing in Finance and Strategy) at the Ross School of Business (University of Michigan) in Ann Arbor, Michigan, USA. He earned his undergraduate degree in business, with an accounting concentration, from North Carolina Central University in Durham, NC. Mr. Asubonten has also earned an Advanced Diploma from the Financial Times (FT) Board of Directors NED program in London.

He has taught Economics, Accounting, and Finance up to the graduate level on the adjunct faculty in two universities in Michigan.

He has served as a board member on both for-profit and not-for-profit entities in various countries.

He is a Certified Public Accountant (CPA), and holds the Chartered Financial Analyst (CFA) designation.

References

Boulton, R.E.S, D. Liebert, and S. Samek. 2000. *Cracking the Value Code: How Successful Businesses Are Creating Wealth in the New Economy.* Arthur Anderson. Harper Business.

Copeland, T., T. Kohler, and J. Murrin. 1990. *VALUATION: Measuring and Managing the Value of Companies.* McKinsey & Company, Inc. John Wiley & Sons.

Charan, R. 2001. *What The CEO Wants You To Know: How Your Company Really Works.* Crown Business. New York.

Charan, R., and N. Tichy: 1998. *Every Business Is a Growth Business: How Your Company Can Prosper Year After Year.* Three Rivers Press. New York

Gadiesh, O., and H. MacArthur. *Lessons From Private Equity Any Company Can Use.* 2008. Bain & Company. Harvard Business Press.

Tichy, N., N. Cardwell. 2002. *The Cycle of Leadership.* HarperCollins. New York.8

Printed in the USA
CPSIA information can be obtained
at www.ICGtesting.com
LVHW021534180923
758505LV00011B/821